Japan As We Lived It

Can East and West ever meet?

By Bernard Krisher

YOHAN PUBLICATIONS INC.

First English edition published in Hong Kong by ASIA 2000 Ltd. 1989
Co-published in Japan by Yohan Publications, Inc., Tokyo, Japan 1989
First published in Japanese by Simul Press, Tokyo, Japan 1985
Copyright© Bernard Krisher, 1989.
All rights reserved.
ISBN 962-7160-07-5
Produced in Hong Kong by ASIA 2000 Ltd.
6th Fl., 146 Prince Edward Road West, Kowloon

I WOULD LIKE TO DEDICATE THIS BOOK TO MY MOTHER AND LATE FATHER. THEIR JOINT SACRIFICE, IN GIVING ME THE LARGER BEDROOM OF OUR NEW YORK APARTMENT WHEN WE EMIGRATED TO THE UNITED STATES FROM GERMANY, IN 1941, ENABLED ME TO INSTALL A MIMEOGRAPH MACHINE AND, AT THE AGE OF TWELVE, TO ESTABLISH MY OWN 'PUBLISHING EMPIRE'. THUS BEGAN MY LIFE-LONG JOURNALISTIC CAREER.

Contents

Contents

Introduction

Foreigners generally go through three stages in their contact with Japan. It is usually love at first sight, followed by a period of disenchantment; finally, one reaches 'satori' or, at least, an accommodation with the society.

The short-term visitor to Japan is enchanted by the graciousness of the Japanese. Everything works, the country is so peaceful, its people so diligent and honest. There is a respect for age. The cities are clean and safe, harmony abounds. And, a foreigner is treated like a king.

But the veneer begins to peel after some months. Japan is, after all, a closed society and the foreigner who has now applied himself to master the language and culture finds himself alienated. He is met by an impenetrable barrier. He is not welcome into the inner circle; his efforts to be more Japanese are not appreciated. His fluent Japanese is reciprocated by replies in pidjin English. He is forever warned to take his slippers off when walking on 'tatami' or perennially complimented on his handling of chopsticks. In daily life he encounters a decided rigidity and squareness. If he breaks the rules the price he pays is a debasing apology. He is never made to forget that he is a foreigner.

One need only read the letters to the editor in Tokyo's English-language dailies to gauge the intensity of neurosis among this group of disenchanted foreigners. Their complaints range from the fingerprinting the government requires of foreign residents to the dearth of English-language programs on TV. But wait. There is still a third group—those foreigners who have survived this stage, usually after residence of more than five years, and who have made their accommodation with Japan. They have discovered that Japan, like any country, has its share of flaws, yet on the whole isn't such a bad society, particularly for foreigners.

So many books are written about Japan nowadays—everything from eliciting the secret of its management techniques to why its women are regarded as second class citizens. I strongly believe the best answers are usually based on personal experience, so I chose this form: inter-

1

Introduction

views with foreigners from the third group, foreigners who have had long contact with Japan. From their rich experiences I have hoped to elicit fresh views and possibly debunk some widely-held myths about this country.

In a sense this book could have been titled "Outsiders on the Inside" but my sense of Japan also taught me that in order to attract attention, a book for the Japanese (as even in English this book in part is) requires certain magic words—like "Nippon" "Dame" or "Tanaka." As I am neither writing about the former prime minister nor debunking anything, "Nihon" (Japan) was essential.

This leads me to another observation: probably no other people are as narcissistic as the Japanese; the possible exception are the Jews. Being Jewish, I have noted this and a number of other cultural similarities which may, in fact, have made it easier for me to understand and feel comfortable in Japan. Both have closed societies and are basically insecure. Both may tend to regard themselves as, in some ways, superior and unique. Both are also extremely hospitable and generous with strangers, though their generosity may also serve as a means to keep outsiders at a distance, to avert them from integrating themselves into the clan. Judaism is the only religion that does not engage in missionary work. Converts are not welcome. Likewise, the attainment of Japanese citizenship is nearly impossible and the requirements are almost absurd—one is forced to adopt a Japanese name! Both Japanese and Jews further seem to view almost everything in terms of whether it is good or bad for them. Thus, though we follow world events closely, we seem to view such occurrences not in the context of their historical sense but rather how they affect us. "Is it good or bad for the Japanese (or Jews)?" This makes us both a rather myopic and provincial people.

So, here I am, like many a perplexed foreigner before me, staring at the Japanese navel. "This nation is the delight of my soul," wrote St. Francis Xavier more than 400 years

2

Introduction

ago when he visited Japan. Three centuries later Lafcadio Hearn said "There is no Japan like Tokyo." Westerners have always been fascinated by Japan and literature abounds with succinct impressions of this country by foreigners. John Gunther, in Inside Asia (1939) commented that "no one in the world is so unintelligent as a single Japanese, and no one is as bright as two."

In the preparation of this book, I searched through memoirs, biographies, essays and collections of letters and compiled a volume of quotations from other foreigners who had encountered Japan before. I would like to share some of their views with you as a point of departure for the collection of my contemporary interviews. Then you can judge whether Japan has changed all that much.

"Japan is essentially a country of paradoxes and anomalies, where all—even familiar things—put on new faces, and are curiously reversed. Except that they do not walk on their hands instead of their feet, there are few things in which they do not seem, by some occult law, to have been impelled in a perfectly opposite direction, and a reversed order. They write from top to bottom, from right to left, in perpendicular instead of horizontal lines; and their books begin where ours end, thus furnishing examples of the curious perfection this rule of contraries has attained. Their locks, though imitated from Europe, are all made to lock by turning the key from left to right. The course of all sublunary things appear reversed. Their day is for the most part our night; and this principle of antagonism crops out in the most unexpected bizarre way in all their moral being, customs and habits. I leave to philosophers the explanation—I only speak to the facts. There old men fly kites while the children look on; the carpenter uses his plane by drawing it to him, and their tailors stitch from them; they mount their horses from the off-side—the horses stand in the stables with their heads where we place their tails, and the bells to their harness are always on the hind quarters instead of the front;

Introduction

ladies black their teeth instead of keeping them white, and their anti-crinoline tendencies are carried to the point of seriously interfering not only with grace of movement but with all locomotion, so tightly are the lower limbs, from the waist downwards, girt round with their garments—and finally, the utter confusion of sexes in the public bath-house, making that correct which we in the West deem so shocking and improper, I leave as I find it—a problem to solve."

Sir Rutheford Alcock, *The Capital of the Tycoon*, 1863.

"Give as little foothold as possible to foreigners."
Herbert Spencer, *Letter to Baron Kaneko Kentaro*, 1892.

"Japan, a country combining a feverish proficiency in many of the habits of advanced civilisation with uncompromising reliefs of feudal crystalization."
George Curzon, *Marquess of Kedleston, Tales of Travel*, 1923.

"The Japanese are the most irreligious people that I have ever seen—their pilgrimages are picnics, and their religious festivals fairs."
Isabella Bird, *Unbeaten Tracks in Japan*, 1880.

"The Japanese have never had a philosophy of their own. Formerly they bowed down before the shrine of Confucius. They now bow down before the shrine of Herbert Spencer."
Basil Hall Chamberlain, *Things Japanese*, 1890.

"As in sex, the Japanese do not care for extended encounters: 'in and out' is their motto in love and war—another example of national insecurity."
James Kirkup, *Heaven and Hara-Kiri*, 1974.

Introduction

How courteous is the Japanese;
He always says, 'Excuse it' please,
He climbs into his neighbor's garden,
And smiles, and says, 'I beg your pardon;'
He bows and grins a friendly grin,
And calls his hungry family in;
He grins, and bows a friendly bow;
'So sorry, this my garden now.'

Ogden Nash, *'Fellow Creatures, II: The Japanese,' in*
I'm a Stranger Here Myself, 1938.

"The inhabitants show a notable wit, and an incredible patience, in suffering, labor and sorrows. They take great and diligent care lest, either in word or deed they should show either fear, or dullness of mind, and lest they should make any man (whosoever he be) partaker of their troubles and wants. They covet exceedingly honor and prayer; and poverty with them bringeth no damage to the nobility of blood. They suffer not the least injury in the world to pass unrevenged. For gravity and courtesy they give not place to the Spaniards. They are generally affable and full of compliments. They are very punctual in the entertaining of strangers, of whom they will curiously inquire even trifles of foreign people, as of their manners, and such like things. They will as soon lose one limb as to omit one ceremony in welcoming a friend."

Anon. *The First Book of Relations of Modern States,*
16th century.

"Tokyo is the city where one encounters at its most intense, its most vital and its most vulgar the kind of society that has resulted from the double impact of industrialization and the West. Japanese society is a kind of conglomerate, in which borrowings from many places at many times are fossilized and united by the cement of Japanese tradition.

Introduction

The writing and much of the surviving religious and courtly ceremonial came from China. The present political constitution is basically British. The beer and the beer halls which one finds in every city are German. The uniform of the students is that of Hapsburg, Austria, and the middy blouses of the high school girls date from Victorian England. The cake shops, when they are not Japanese, are most often French in style, the coffee bars are Italian-innocent emanations of La Dolce Vita—and the fashions in Western dress are American. As for art, the styles run all the way from the French impressionists to the most recent schools of New York and Italy, and often we would be impressed against our better judgments by the meticulous faithfulness with which Japanese painters had imitated such masters as Monet, Matisse, and Picasso.

At first we were bewildered at the very incongruity of this mixture of the strange and the familiar, and then amazed at the zest for having the best of both worlds which seems to be the most outstanding characteristic of the modern Japanese."

George Woodcock, *Asia Gods and Cities*, 1966.

There has always been a temptation among foreign observers, particularly journalists, to project the future course of Japan. The temptation has been to predict that Japan would turn increasingly Western; that it would abandon its old values and customs, pay less attention to the work ethic, respect for the aged, diminish the importance of education—and in another context, flex its international muscle, re-militarize.

In my view, the more you read what observers have written in the past about Japan, the more one finds how little the society has really changed. It's remarkable how many of the Japanese traits uncovered in a book written in the sixteenth century still hold today.

6

Introduction

Taxi drivers abroad often ask me questions about Japan when they learn that I live there. A most frequent one is whether the Japanese aren't going to change some day and abandon all those diligent traits to become more like us (and consequently help reduce the trade frictions by becoming lazier). My answer is that Japan, like all vital societies, changes. So, Japan is constantly changing and, fortunately or unfortunately, following into many of our footsteps. Yet, while America rushes head-on at 150 miles an hour in whatever new direction she pursues, the Japanese more cautiously and slowly move at, perhaps, only 30 miles an hour. Thus the gap always remains. If America and the rest of the world is evolving a less manageable society, so is Japan, but at a slower pace, so she will always retain the advantage.

Enough. I am upstaging the group of wise contemporaries, myself included (one of the perks of orchestra-ting a book is that you can if you choose put yourself in it), whose observations on Japan as "outsiders on the inside" is what this book is about. I welcome you to share these informal conversations with us, using what Donald Richie further on calls the technique of a "ruminating beast" to munch and graze on our experiences.

In closing, may I say how honored I am that Simul Press chose to publish the original Japanese edition of this book long before I could find an English language publisher. I have had a long relationship with Simul International, especially with Mr. Tamura, the president of Simul, who published my first (and favorite) book on Japan, Interview, which consisted of major interviews with Asian personalities of the sixties and early seventies. I have always been impressed with Mr. Tamura's editorial genius, which is reflected in the prestige which the publishing arm of Simul now enjoys and proven in the many distinguished titles now on the Simul list.

Donald Richie

"We're seeing a dinosaur-like structure still surviving...it's astonishing. We're privileged to live inside the dinosaur, but you know what happens to dinosaurs."

Japan as We Lived It

Bernard Krisher: Why did you first come to Japan?

Donald Richie: I first came to Japan at the end of 1946. The reason I came was not anything so positive as coming to Japan. The war was over. Those of us who'd been in the war simply didn't feel like going back and going to school. We wanted to get further out in the world. I discovered the occupation authorities needed people. So, I was interviewed and brought over here as a clerk typist.

Once here, I was put to work in an office, but the occupation was so fluid that I was able to move around. Eventually, I moved to the *Stars & Stripes*, where I was able to return to some activities that I myself wanted, such as film, for example. I was there as a sort of entertainment editor/film critic for four years, until 1949.

I wasn't moving toward anything concrete when I came here. I was actually running away from something, like the farm in Ohio. But, once here in Japan, I don't believe I was here for a week before I realized that this was something extraordinary and that I was seeing something the world has never seen before: the collision of cultures which occurred here after the war. I was so intrigued by the spectacle that I wanted to stay here, to be witness, so I could see, write about and consequently comprehend and understand what it was I was seeing.

What I was seeing was the mighty spectacle of a culture absolutely changing gears before my very eyes, something that hadn't happened since the Greek and the Persians got together. A cultural bargain, a symbiosis. It was really quite collosal and is quite collosal. It's still going on.

And so, I had a grandstand seat to watch this, and this was certainly one of the reasons why I was fascinated by the country, by the change that was going on, and why I am still fascinated by it.

BK: Have you been here continuously since 1946?

DR: Pretty much now. There have been seasons when I've been gone. The longest period was between 1968 and 1975, when I was the curator of film at the Museum of

Modern Art in New York; but, even so, I managed it so I would leave in May and return in November. I spent all the summer months here.

BK: What made you go back to New York and what made you come back here?

DR: Well, I went back to New York, because in my field, which is film history and film scholarship, there is no position of greater acumen, no better position than the curator of film at the Museum of Modern Art. I was honored to have been chosen to occupy the post, and you just don't say no to anything like that. And once you get there, and if you like film, you suddenly realize: this is the largest electric train a boy ever had; you can do anything you want to. You can really do great constructive work and I liked all of that.

While I was there, I did nothing except work for the Museum. I'd wake up at six in the morning, be there by seven, stay there until around ten at night, get home by eleven. I paid no attention whatsoever to life in New York because life in the Museum was so attractive. Beyond that, I would have done so anyway, even if it had been lousy work, because life in New York terrified me so. I had not been used to it, although I went to school there and I'd been there during the war. I had changed and things had changed to the extent that it wasn't anything I knew about anymore. I was an absolute alien in my own culture. I didn't know how to make the city work. I didn't know how to do anything. I wanted to run back here, to a country I knew better than my own, as it turned out. You see, I was gone from America from 1946 to, can you imagine, 1968. What happened then? I missed all the manifestations that were going on in my own country. So, Japan became much more easily understandable to me than America.

And so, it was these two things, one that kept me there, and one that eventually made me come back. I was eligible for directorship. They told me that I was going to be a director and I did not want to be director and everything that it meant. I didn't want to go through life committing myself to nothing. So, I said no, and they said yes, and I said no: I'll remain the curator, and they said we're collapsing the job slot. So, I said, in that case, I'll go, and that's why I left.

BK: What have you gotten out of your Japan experience? What are the key things?

DR: Oh, Jesus! Well, I suppose, I live here. What I've gotten out of it has to do with life and philosophy and how to live. The thing that Japan has taught me, I guess, that's the most important to me, is that there is always an alternate method of thought. There is always a way other than the ones I was taught as a child, caught in the amber of my own time, in Ohio in the thirties and forties. That things need not be dualistic. That dichotomies are not the only answer, though they may be part of the answer. That there are alternate ways of doing things, alternate ways of considering. There are parallels.

This is what life on the sliding scale of Japan has taught me: it's loosened me up, it's softened me, it's made me more human. The rigidities to which I was subjected as a child have failed to solidify. I have not become the kind of person I was probably slated to become because of what I have experienced here.

Also, for anybody who likes Japan, it helps a great deal if you don't have too high an opinion of where you came from. I don't refer to America so much as I refer to a small town in Ohio in a certain period of time, which I have no feeling for and never did have much. Mine was a classic case. Usually they went to New York; I came half the way around the world to here instead.

When I say "I don't have too high an opinion of where I came from," I mean I don't have a strong feeling of "us" and "them"; "us" being people back in Ohio. Also, being the kind of character I am has helped a great deal, in that I don't have too high an opinion of myself. I've a very high opinion of my capabilities but I don't trust my emotions particularly. They get in my way. I don't really trust how I feel, although I tend to trust what I think. I've gotten to the point where I truly believe now that, in regard to myself, if I cry, it's not because I'm sad. I am sad because I cry. First comes the crying, then the sadness. These are things, the emptiness at the heart of the onion, the emptiness of the mirror—a pleasing thing. This has been taught to me by the people I have chosen to live among. So, Japan has had a very strong effect in making me the kind of person I've become.

BK: Do you think the Japanese understand all that?

DR: No, I don't think they understand any of it. This is a good example of something which is absolutely natural, which is going on beneath the surface of every day life.

Occasionally, cultural differences will show up. Then people I'm speaking with, Japanese, will suddenly realize that something is different between their approach and mine. But, on the whole, they are so busy attempting to capture as realistically as possible the surface of my life as a Westerner, the surface of Western life, that they remain very much ignorant of what is going on in their own depths.

BK: In fact, how perceptive, or introspective, are the Japanese?

DR: I think it is to their credit that they're not introspective at all. The Japanese are good existential people. They may give mouth credence to other beliefs, but, if you watch a group of Japanese, you will realize that the existential thesis is at work. A person is what he does, not what he intends to do. Put action where the mouth is. People act here and people tend to act as though they believe that action is after all the deciding factor, not intention. America, I must say, still remains the land of good intentions—which pave the way to hell, among other things. Somebody also once said that the only religion the Japanese had was the religion of being Japanese, which has superceded all other possible religions, Shinto, Buddhist, Christian. I think that's true. Anybody that prescribes to something like this is guilty of bad faith to a degree, but I'm not talking about great collective delusions. I'm talking about person to person matters. Are they introspective? No, they are not.

Japan as We Lived It

BK: Do the Japanese have principles? Are they guided by some values or is everything case by case?

DR: They are guided by a system of values which says that everything must be done case by case. Case by case certainly exists, however loosely, in other systems too. But the fundamental belief of the Japanese is that case by case will be determined by nobody else than the Japanese. Right?

Love of nature, one of the underpinnings of the value system, is to be understood only if you look to how nature is defined. The way the Japanese define nature is as something that we have just finished touching up. So, the Japanese garden is not the wild garden. The 18th century wilderness garden of England would not be admired here at all. Instead, you must move the rock for some reason or another two feet, then back, and when you've finished restructuring everything, nobody but the trained eye will be able to tell the difference. That doesn't make any difference. The important thing is that it's been touched, that nature has been touched by the hand of man, specifically, by a Japanese hand.

This is true of all so-called natural things. People sometimes ask me: "Well, how can you say the Japanese feel so strongly about nature, and love it so much? Look at what they've done to the country. There isn't a port that isn't absolutely ruined. The ecological damage in this country is collosal. What's all this love of nature?" My answer is that nature has been defined, and so, the hand of the Japanese, if its moving for aesthetic purposes, will make the garden and the tea-house, but the same hand has many purposes, and if it is used for economic purposes, then it will say "Oh, yes, this full, beautiful harbor must be taken away. This is absolutely the best place to make *Mutsu* a home." And, so, naturally, this takes precedence.

It is the same hand, but the purposes of the hand are different. You can't say that the Japanese are particularly contradictory in doing this. You can't say that a person who loves nature would never do such a thing. It's not the way it goes. You have to define why the Japanese touch everything.

Donald Richie

They are an amazing people. Everything that enters their ken must be captured, examined, turned around this way, squeezed, turned into something. If it is going to be used, it's going to be turned into something very Japanese and we won't recognize it after a while. If it's not to be used, it will be rejected out of hand, from where it will not surface again.

What do you call a people like that? All people are like that. This is called civilization, right? But only the Japanese are this way so much. This runs into what people ought to be paying more attention to when writing books about the Japanese. It isn't that the Japanese are so much different from other people; it's that they're so much more apparent. The Japanese show, with innocent-like guile, what other civilizations are busy sweeping under the carpet. The Japanese feeling for reality is such that if it exists that is reason enough for showing it. While they are manipulating nature, they do not really manipulate. They don't hide their reasons for doing things. Take their architecture, all the supports are there and visible. A facade is not necessary in classical Japanese architecture. Indeed, you don't want it. In the same way, classical Japanese dress and the way of life, you can see all supports. You can see how it's made. Things are apparent in this country.

BK: It's been said that the Japanese have a great sense of beauty and are also oblivious to ugliness. That touches on what you said, but Tokyo is probably by all accounts the ugliest major city in the world as far as landmarks. The streets are unwieldy, the overhead passes are horribly, metallically discoloured and so on. And yet, you have in the corner of some street a temple or a nice garden or something behind a wall.

DR: That's true. Right in the middle of what we would call ugliness, you have this little piece of beauty. A lot of this has to do with the extraordinary selective vision of the Japanese. It always proceeds to the particular. The particular is the most important form. We in the West like generalities, which is why I am now speaking in generalities. We like the wide view. It shows us where we are, the open vista and things like this. The West, which has given us philosophy, science, rubrics, is still fond of these things and believes that this is a viable view of the world.

If you move as in a Hitchcock film you have to move from the general to the particular. This is the continual movement of thought in the West. In Asia, and certainly in Japan, you see the same thing in reverse. Everything is a detail. In fact, if you get a general view, it seems to be terribly mixed up because the Japanese are not particularly good in putting small details together in any meaningful way. You have a jumble, which may be very human, like in Tokyo itself, which is a jumble of little towns, no plans at all. They are not very good at logical discourse either, which is not to their purpose, but is to ours.

The Kurosawa method, as opposed to the Hitchcock method, is to the particular and then, very slowly, to an ordered generality, perhaps.

So, with the Kurosawan view of the world you can see that the Japanese have an extraordinary, highly developed form of selectivity in their vision. They will instantly pick up the beautiful thing and then disregard all the ugliness and horror that surrounds it.

This selectivity really goes beyond something the Westerner understands, as, when you go to somebody's house or a bar, you can find that the television, the record player, the radio and a loud conversation are all going on simultaneously. To us it sounds like chaos. To the Japanese, with an attuned sensitivity and the ability to follow all these at a given level, this is not the case.

What is beautiful, what is ugly, is further complicated because in Japan we have a double culture. We have the Western which is Japanese. Then we have the Eastern, which is also Japanese. We have these things going on together and the Japanese cannons of what is beautiful and what is not, are still known pretty much. So, there's a sort of consensus, which goes back to the sixteenth, seventeenth centuries as to

16

what constitutes a flower arrangement, a *kakujiki*, a well-proportioned tea ceremony.

Japan got Western things but our Western consensus on what makes things beautiful is missing. Consequently we accuse the Japanese of bad taste in Western things: the mock Fontainbleau effects of the *Geihinkan*, the Akasaka Prince Hotel. They're incredibly ugly because the ideas which govern our nexus of what is beautiful and what is not, is missing. The aesthetic argument here in Japan about beauty becomes very complicated because of this, I think.

BK: Staying on the question of the Japanese mind, in the era of communications, the *honne* and *tatemae* of communicating, how would you say this fits into the Japanese character? Why is there a dual system of communicating? Why don't they just say it the way it is? Why do they have to go through such a *kabuki*?

DR: Of course, the more one looks abroad and then looks back, is to realize again that all cultures have *honne* and *tatemae*, but only the Japanese have names for them. That's interesting. The very fact that in the West we have to say "say it like it is," the very fact that such a phrase is necessary, indicates that at sometime or other "saying it like it isn't" is prevalent, right?

Again, it is very Western, I think, that we would then take this and turn it into something very positive like "saying it like it is," as being the only good thing to do. But you notice about *honne* and *tatemae*, that this polarity lives very happily with itself.

There is never any indication on the part of the Japanese that one is better than the other. We in the West would tend to say that "let it all hang out" is a good thing, and "being uptight" is a bad thing. This is one of the articles of our faith. The idea of having two things, which we consider antithetical, going on simultaneously, irritates us, that is because, despite our claims, we are not an intellectually dynamic people.

Dynamism of two apparently antithetical things existing

at once is Eastern and considerably Japanese. It's as if an electrical current, a feeling, is going on between these two things all the time. If you settle for one of them, you've cut the circuit.

I think this is one of the reasons for the tremendous energy of the Japanese. If we take William James' theory that we are dynamos anyway, that we have coils of wire around us, then, it fits. If you have two unresolved things, of which the resolvability is not even considered, and put them side by side, you get a tremendous amount of energy. Look through Japanese life and you will find a great many opposites standing side by side, things which are antithetical.

Buddhism and Shinto are absolutely antithetical and yet they are mutually entertained. The fact that they are mutually entertained would make one wonder to the extent either is entertained, if at all.

In the case of *honne* and *tatemae*, one sees that these things are entertained in this way, but they are not interiorized as they are in the West. I mean, we believe in sin, for example, because our forefathers got after us and instilled this in us; we're imprinted. The Japanese don't believe in sin.

Do the Japanese believe in *honne* and *tatemae*?

Had they ever heard of *giri ninjo*, I wonder, until Benedict wrote about it?

Judging by their actions, no; judging by their literature, they know about it, of course, but the thing is, they do not interiorize these things. So, *honne* and *tatemae* become tools. They become things to use. The *tatemae* is used just as we use it. Emily Post wrote a whole book about *tatemae* in a way, right? Miss Manners continues. But we institutionalize that sort of thing, whereas they don't.

In America for example, people say "Well, I have done this , I have done that." And they will touch themselves on the breast as though there was deep down the real *me*, some little being lurking under there someplace who could be uncovered somehow. As though the real them was all covered up by something, you know.

Donald Richie

That we aren't who we are is so common to Western thought, particularly in America. We don't even realize the idiocy of it. This sort of thing comes from believing that there is something hidden underneath all of us, the *honne*, the real thing. *Tatemae* is the surface we've got to get rid of.

I'm saying that the Japanese do not think like that. I'm saying that they would not more consider the real them lurking than they would really consider having a soul. There's no word for soul. There's *tamashi*, which is a sort of light that goes on over graveyards.

BK: If you look at the way people act in politics, for example, you had Mondale in the last election saying "You get what you see." That was his slogan. Can you imagine a Nakasone saying that?

DR: I certainly cannot.

BK: In Japan, they campaign with white gloves on top of trucks, say *yoroshiku onegai shimasu* , and people vote for that.

DR: That's right, exactly so. People vote for that. Roland Barthes is right, it's a system of signs. But he said the signifier was empty. It's not empty at all. All these signs mean something. All these elements of *tatemae* are something. The mask is the face because that is all there is. We've been calling 'face' the wrong thing all the time. A face is really a mask, and when the Japanese talk about their *honne* and their own true *kimochi*, they're not talking about something that is hidden from view really. They're talking about things that they don't often put to use. But this is a land certainly where *tatemae* and its elaborate system of signals and signs is used with increasing efficiency.

BK: How have you changed, yourself, in the thirty to forty years of contact that you've had with Japan in utilizing some of these symbols? How much *giri ninjo*, and how much *honne, tatemae* is there in you in dealing with fellow foreigners or with Japanese?

DR: Not very much. You see, what happens is that we all get imprinted by our cultures by the time we're two or three,

19

when almost all the values are set. If I didn't watch myself, I would fall into the trap that a lot of foreigners fall into in this country of being more American than the Americans.

You know, the ill-will displayed by these people in the readers column of the *Japan Times,* for example, is astonishing. Why are they so full of ill-will? They're reacting. They're becoming more and more what they think they were back home.

I fight that battle all the time. the famous we-them battle, or the I-them battle, because it is beside the point. If you're doing this sort of thing, then you're not doing your proper work.

So, have I changed? I'm afraid not very much. But, even if I haven't changed much as a person, what has changed very much is me as a spectator, as an observer. I am aware of this. What Japan has taught me is self-awareness and it's taught me that the kind of inbuilt directions and old tapes that I came with aren't the only ones.

BK: But, you know, foreigners are either unwilling, unable or uninterested in integrating too much into Japanese life or culture. Even if they wanted to, they would find the door pretty much shut. Conversely, America is a different kind of culture. People do assimilate very easily into American culture. If you have a Japanese living in America for more than five years, he cannot even come back here and be recognized as a Japanese. He will have lost a great deal. What distinguishes our two cultures so?

DR: In America, the only way to live happily is to join. Can you imagine a Japanese living like a Japanese in America for a long period of time? It doesn't happen. They come back or commit suicide or something. America demands that you join and there's a great deal to be said about that.

Japan, on the other hand, forbids you to join if you're a foreigner, as you know. You can never get to become part of the *nakama*. If you're white, you get kicked up to the white ghetto. If you're yellow, you get kicked down to a lower echelon ghetto. You're in a ghetto, no matter what. The ghetto might have a terrific view—I wouldn't change it for anything— but it's a ghetto to the extent that I can't go out and jump right into the nitty gritty.

So, people who are here are discouraged from becoming Japanese, and people who live there are told if you are not like us, you are not going to stay here.

Also, I must say, to live like an American has a great number of advantages. I've known for many years: if I were Japanese, I wouldn't stay in this country for ten minutes.The weight of this society on a person who is Japanese is very heavy. The police state is very much alive for Japanese, not for us. If I were Japanese, I would either go into *mizu shobai*, or kill myself or I don't know what I'd be, but I wouldn't be a good citizen, I know that.

The Japanese who go abroad suddenly have this pressure lifted. For the ones who are successfully living in America, at least the egalitarianism of America is most appealing. It's just the opposite of what we have in Japan, right?

BK: Well, that raises two questions. One is why are the Japanese so closed to foreigners? And, corrolary to that I suppose, why don't the Japanese manage very well when they are let loose, outside the constraints of their own society?

DR: Yes, they manage very, very badly. But let me try and find answer to your first question.

Talking about civilization means talking about people being imprinted early. Civilization is imprinted very early too in America. Even though centuries have gone by, you still see Americans pursuing happiness, even though it's not exactly something one can do now—though perhaps you could in '70 or '76. So, in the same way here, you find people reacting much like in the early Edo period. You know, closed, rigid minds, minds on rails which know all the bureaucratic answers. You find all of this in great abundance here because cultural imprintation is a strong thing.

Most cultures, most people, unless they are a mongrel

nation like America or unless they are a very brave nation, which the Americans also are, tend to repress their individuals. It makes things so much easier. You know, Germany before the war for instance or benign repressive societies like Sweden is now. This fits the man on the street very well because, in existential terms, he doesn't have to do very much. He goes along. In Sweden they go along. You can't make any more money, because of the tax, but still, they go along. And so, people tend to like governments which make up their minds about things. In that way, Japan is no different from anybody else.

Now, if you live under such a repressive, let's call it repressive, regime, then what happens when you are suddenly released? It happens all the time with children. Very well behaved children are allowed to go to their grandmother's. Liberty Hall! Jelly beans! The child goes to pieces, has stomach ache and squally tantrums and is brought back home in disgrace. I think that that's what happens to people from strong regimes when they go to countries with less structured regimes.

Remember in *Ninotchka* where Garbo laughs? It's all about that. Discovering silk stockings. The Japanese who go out in their crocodiles and behave very badly on the streets are rude, unthinking. They're people who are engaged in saturnalia. They are behaving like servants at the servants ball. They're over-reacting.

BK: You get one extreme in the war in the way they treated prisoners.

DR: Exactly.

BK: And the other is respect for order at home, which is prevalent now. Thus the fact that terrorism has no fertile ground in Japan. So those Japanese intent on practicing it, have had to go abroad. You have the Red Army in the Middle East.

DR: There are many, many symptoms from all over.

BK: Or, again, businessmen enjoying themselves in South East Asia.

DR: That's right. You get the same thing here, inside the country, as well as outside, but inside the country, it's trammeled. What else are the festivals, for example? The *Sanja Matsuri* for example, which is a legal blow up. There is any amount of things within the society which you can do, things which are tolerated in the society. For example, you can make mini-saturnalias for people. I think that's all to be put to the credit, or the ill credit, of a society which is this rigid.

BK: But the rigidity is not imposed from above. It's one of the few self-disciplined or self-repressive societies, isn't it? Legally, you can go out and be just as free as anyone in the world. You can say what you want. Where does this come from?

DR: In our culture we have God and we have our conscience, and we have the idea of sin. We self-institutionalize this, so that even if you are all alone in the room, God is still looking at you. So, in other words, we have imprinted ourselves with this. Our form of self-censorship has to do entirely with interior things. We don't need another person outside to look at us.

In Japan we find people who do exactly the same thing, but do it socially. They have decided to limit themselves, to censor themselves, not because God is looking and not because they are looking, but because other people are looking.

A good example recently is the Diet member, an elderly gentleman, who happened to pick up a young girls magazine and was shocked. And so he said we must put a stop to this, and he was very well placed, so he managed to put a stop to it and other things, including outside advertising for porno theaters, *nozoki beya*, and such things going on in various sections of the town, particularly in Shinjuku.

Now, there was no motion, except some vague talk about changing the law, which probably won't be done, but what happened was that everyone in these businesses instantly began to self- censor himself. As you know, the magazines all of a sudden stopped running these articles which had upset the Diet member. All the theaters in Tokyo that had been showing these porno films, removed the objectionable posters and replaced them by hand tooled things just giving the names, followed several weeks later by printed ones. The *nozoki beya* instantly took off all their pictures, just leaving the name to indicate what was there. The cops didn't say they had to do this yet everybody did it. Japanese films, for example, have a board of censorship, but it's called self-censorship. There's nothing official about it. The companies or their proxies come together and look at all the films and decide where to blot out this, and where to put the bouncing ball. This is all done because it has been turned into the body collective, in precisely the same way that we in the West turn it into the body single. It makes perfect sense. It's done for exactly the same reasons: control. In both cases, there is something controlling. For us, it is the power of the Western church and the entire governmental control apparatus, *Tokugawa* tradition is controlling it here.

BK: And they certainly don't want to be ostracized from their own village.

DR: They certainly don't want to be ostracized. *Mura hachibu*, ostracization is the worst thing that can happen, even now. You read Heian literature and you're a little bit bemused at the way people really carry on being sent ten miles down the road. So what? People in Canterbury wouldn't have felt this way. But the idea is not so much as being taken away from Kyoto, as you're being kicked out of the *nakama*. You're no longer a member of good standing. This is the worst punishment, it is said, that a Japanese can possibly have. Now who came up which this extraordinary thing? I don't know, it's been going a long time.

BK: Can Japan continue to live indefinitely in this garden of whatever you want to call it? Paradise?

Certainly the rest of the world is putting a lot of pressure on Japan.

Japan has been protected in the last three or four decades

largely by the United States, both in their economy and defense. This won't last forever.

DR: Yes, America even arranged for the Vietnam and the Korean Wars, which Japan made much money on.

Things are cracking left and right. You feel like you're on the avalanche when the sheet ice is threatening to come apart. Basic things that I though I'd never see change are changing.The diet. I thought food was pretty basic and no matter what else, nonetheless, *ochazuke* was here to stay. Well, it's not.The diet is changing very, very rapidly. The body frames of people are changing.

I thought, well, at least, our old friend the escalator, that carries you from kindergarten on up to the grave, will not change. But no, it's stopping all over the place. Someone's dismantling it, and I'm sure only the government, maybe the *Mombusho*, will still have it going.

The thing which has not changed though, and I thought one time of writing a book on this, is the pattern of, the way of thought. The way of looking at things. The way in which the brain makes its way to its conclusions. But, of course, these are deep things. These will change last.

For example, logic, *ronri, ronriteki*, still remains one of the dirtiest words in the language. Sure, a lot of its dirtiness means it can be used effectively politically to shout down your opponent. On the other hand, it is really felt by the Japanese that if B follows A and is followed by C and therefore C follows A, the conclusion is something which is so profoundly beyond anybody's point that the only possible use it can have is to show how you happened to reach it. But, if you've reached a certain conclusion, action being all, it doesn't make any difference how you reached it.

Instead, if you look at reality and you look at the brain as it really is, you will find that it is a ruminating beast that goes around and munches and grazes and its movement is circular. It moves by association, and this is the way the Japanese think. They think associatively, as you've seen many, many a time.

We are trying painfully to make some kind of linear structure out of our experience and nothing we say will make any sense because the Japanese person we're talking with is ruminating in a circular fashion, where one thing suggests another and another.

If we say that's wrong, we're going to have hell, because this happens to be the way the Japanese brain works. So, Japanese art, Japanese novels are entirely associative. Japanese movies are associative. Anything the Japanese mind creates is associative. It lacks structure. It lacks linearity, which is why scientists have to use English to talk back and forth. Anything that has our linear motif cannot use Japanese, because we show our patterns in our words.

In daily conversation, these really basic ways of getting at ideas have not changed at all. So, this will be one of the things in 1984 that has not changed. But, when I think of the things that have changed since 1946, and you take an equivalent amount of time and change and add it on to this year till the year 2000 and something, then it is conceivable that Japanese civilization has disappeared. Civilizations do disappear. You can conceive a terminal civilization, a civilization that reaches a point of perfection and stays there until it's stopped. The Mayan and the Aztecs were like that and to an extent the Japanese are like that too.

BK: OK.If you take the thesis that civilizations have to adapt to the times and change or they will be destroyed, and if you accept the other thesis that everything Japan has done up to now has been very good for Japan, then what would you change without threatening the system?

So far, Japan has done quite well for herself. Even the mistake of getting into the war seems to have benefitted her through what she gained by losing. And here we are today in 1984. Japan may be or may not be at the crossroads, but she still is a supposedly harmonious society with decent economic growth, a life-long employment system and so on. Social security, welfare is all taken care of by this corporate kind of stability.

At the same time there are these continuing pressures from a world which is bursting apart as a result of its problems, a world alien to Japan. If Japan is slow to react, will she be hurt? In other words, must Japan change? Should she change? Will she change? Is internationalization the answer? And can the Japanese really become internationalized?

DR: I think that change, as the Japanese have indicated, and as they have proved over the last hundred years, is the only answer. The other answer, going back into seclusion, is unfortunately denied. They're out in the ocean. They must sink or swim, and they're showing a great aptitude for swimming. But, then, they've had time to do so, and now, time is catching up. Future shock is upon them. Will they be allowed to have time?

Time is crucial to the Japanese way of doing things. The people are slow learners. The way of making decisions by consensus takes time. The idea of going from desk to desk and people adding their *hanko*, all of this takes time. The way that the Japanese collectively do anything takes a great deal of time. The Japanese digestive system is very slow. They swallow something and it comes out as something perfectly, marvelously Japanese, eventually, but it takes a long time to go through the system. If they cannot move faster, they cannot cope, that's true.

If we look using Spengler's theory, the zenith is now over Japan and is moving on. It's already been long past America, of course.

Given what Japan has elected to do—it's elected to become a massive industrial community on an economy which can only support about half of its people—if the oil lines are cut, one third of them will die. This dependence on imported energy doesn't seem very farsighted on their part, but what is the alternative? All you can say is this: if Japan does change, it will survive. If it doesn't, it won't.

As the world becomes more brutish, what will count, more and more, is what we have basically: the amount of land and the amount of power we have. Japan doesn't have anything.

BK: Then what does change mean for Japan? Change could mean becoming a military power, or change could mean caving in to some stronger power that blackmailed it.

DR: You're quite right. Change means everything. What does one see for Japan? What does one see for the world?

How something as efficient and well-run as Japan can continue in an increasingly chaotic world, I don't know. As of now, I feel I am in a privileged position of being in a time machine, and I can escape from the chaos of the twentieth century by living in the nineteenth century here.

It's OK to walk down the street. I can walk anywhere at night in one of the biggest cities in the world. The banks don't cheat me. All the telephones work. This is astonishing in the twentieth century that there is a country still like this.

BK: But, that's internal. Japan works very well internally, but they can't translate these internal rules when they are dealing with the wolves in the rest of the world.

DR: That's why I say nineteenth century.

BK: So, basically, Japan has to protect this internal greenhouse or paradise against the enemies without.

DR: And I do not think Japan can do so, because in order to do so, it will have to make so many concessions. It's made so many concessions already. Being successful internationally is the only answer. Eleanor Roosevelt is right; that's the only answer; but getting there, that's the problem.

BK: What are the things Japan should do to become more internationalized? Put more foreign people in its universities? Have more people invited?

DR: People, I think just people, that's the only answer. To pick up government endeavour at any level is no answer. More and more money should be made available for more Japanese to live abroad and then to come back, and for more foreigners to come in here, then go back or stay. An amalgamation of people is the only possible answer.

Donald Richie

BK: Should Japan integrate more foreigners into its society?

DR: It will have to. For every foreigner integrated into its society, it would have one more spokesman, as it were, in another country. They become that much more interrelated.

BK: For example, there were headlines the other day that Japan has finally decided to permit foreigners to work in the government and it turned out that they could deliver mail.

DR: Yes. For a people that for many years now have not wanted to be understood, have actively wanted to be inscrutable, you can imagine! There are going to be so many fights and squabbles about this among the Japanese themselves. You know they say that Japan opened its door to Perry. Japan didn't open its door to Perry. Perry forced a crack in the door, and it's still a crack. There's no open door policy.

BK: If you could make a blueprint, if you were on an advisory committee for internationalizing Japan, or foreign integration into Japan, what would you have foreigners do in Japan that they are not allowed to, or somehow not very tempted to?

DR: Well, I certainly have two minds about this, because I like Japan, even though I know if I were Japanese I wouldn't live here. Nonetheless, I'm very much inclined to keep it as it is, warts and all, because as it is, it still has something which is absolutely its own, unique, vital, which will be the first thing to go. However, to be more constructive about it, I think that the foreigners who come ought to be first of all taught about Japan. I think the direction they're going in now is the right one.

It's the opposite of Meiji. In Meiji, they came over here to teach foreign ways. Japanese know all about foreign ways. They know more about foreign ways than Westerners do. What Westerners ought to do is come over here, but I don't mean as pupils. They shouldn't come over only to study business methods. They should study what I've been talking about: pluralities, ways of thought, look into the idea of nature as something handmade. There's an awful lot that the West could probably learn—not that it's going to—but we're speaking ideally. So, ideally, we would have our governments investing a lot of money in high calibered, artistic people and finding out about Japanese philosophy, Japanese attitudes towards civilization, group people looking at nature. It's very visionary. It's not going to happen, but, ideally, yes.

BK: What about Japanese education?

DR: I would collapse the whole system. The system, as you know, is hopelessly corrupt, and worse, it's turned into some kind of Frankenstein monster running itself. It's programed itself and is now continuing to make certain it goes on. I would collapse it entirely.

I would close Tokyo University for the duration. Anything which has Number One written on it can't be any good. It's like the big tree in the forest. All it can do is kill the other trees. So, I would make certain that all universities were just about equal. This is ideal. People would say, my son's this kind of person, so maybe Waseda would be better, or maybe Nichida would be better, or my son's a real dope, so send him to Hosei. I would have people think like that and I would have the schools much enlarged so there'd be a lot of room for everybody. And there wouldn't be these horrible examination systems going on.

Also, I would change their national character of thought. As an American, I have begun to realize that not everybody has to go to school. Only smart people have to go to school. So, I would insist upon a very healthy, purely sixteenth century elitist way of thought, which I think a country sacrifices at its own peril. Naturally, some people are smarter than others, some people are better than others. England has never forgotten that, although, despite this, it's gone down the drain.

The Japanese put conformity on as an attractive uniform to wear if you want to make money. We must fight against that. If we have an economic reason for being uniform, we're in very great trouble. Even Tokugawa never had that. That was not the reason for the uniform. Obedience was the reason for the uniform. To make money out of wearing it and conforming seems pretty suspicious.

BK: What about languages? Is the English language ability of the Japanese an important factor in the future?

DR: Since not many foreigners are going to learn Japanese, and since communication is important, yes. The weaker and smaller country has to do the language learning of the larger and stronger country. The fact that the Japanese cannot and do not speak foreign languages is a great myth, of course. Given the proper incentive, they can learn as fast as anybody else, and they do. The teaching methods, of course, are hopeless. The reason may be that they do not want to make mistakes in front of their equals and their classmates.

But who says this? Teachers say this. By themselves, the kids don't care. They make mistakes like crazy, and, in fact, I think that all the English learning that is done is by kids together after class, away from the teacher, getting together to try it out and make mistakes. I hear them all the time, but you never hear them in class. It's the teacher and his dumbness, and the fact that he'll get into trouble if the school authorities can prove what everybody knows, that he can't speak English himself. He's as much a victim of the system as the students are.

BK: What would you suggest as a way of improving the teaching system?

DR: Well, I would suggest first of all a system of examinations and licenses with different requirements, and there would be at least one native speaker on every panel. Unless someone could read and write and speak and show familiarity with the language, as indeed is common practice every place else in the world, he would not receive his teaching license. It's crazy. What you have now is akin to a man trying to teach motor boat racing when he doesn't know how to drive a boat!

Japan as We Lived It

BK: What about Japanese myths? In the West, one believes that Japan is a country of total harmony and consensus; that the people get along very well, in companies, etc. You've worked in a Japanese company. Is this true? Do the Japanese get along so well? Is there no back-stabbing, no political rivalries? Or do they just do it differently?

DR: I think the Japanese think they get along better with each other than any other people in the world. Therefore, they think that in smaller groups, such as companies and schools, they do have greater harmony. So, looking in as a foreigner on the outside of that, I would say that, since they do think that, therefore they do. That is, they bend backward, they don't explode where they might otherwise.

On the other hand, looking at what actually does go on, the back-biting, the back-stabbing, it is very difficult to see how, in some instances, people can continue to believe that the Japanese get along better. But everyone has selective vision. You see what you want to see and you believe what you want to believe. So, to the Japanese defending the system, these are all exceptions to the basic rule, which is that the Japanese since they aim at the big *Wa* tend to hit it. They have a point. In the West, after all, we don't aim at it at all, and that would be one of the reasons why we don't hit it at all.

BK: How come then that things suddenly become visible, like Okada bounced from Mitsukoshi? Tanaka went to jail for one night. Right?

DR: There is a pattern, which you notice over the years. In its most clinical and simplest form there is a person who will put up with a great deal, even smilingly. He will put up with indignity heaped upon him one after the other, and one day, far in the future, he will suddenly pick up a sushi knife and go berserk, explode.

Just as people explode, so too do organizations and systems. You can overpower a system to the extent that, all of a sudden, it blows up overnight. Or a very closely knit firm like Mitsukoshi will go on and on and on and on and all of a sudden, a threshold is reached. We don't know where it is, but all these people working for something all of a sudden, appearances being the reverse, start working in opposite directions.

It suddenly seems, and more than that, it's understood that they've put their oars in different directions. It may be counter-productive. It happens in schools, it occurs all the time.

BK: Why does it occur in some situations and not others? Has someone gone to an extreme? Is there a limit beyond which such a reaction is set in motion?

DR: As with people, there is always a limit. So, organizations also have their limits. I don't think it would ever happen with the *Mombusho*. It has limitless patience. But, I can imagine something more volatile, where more volatile people are involved. I think it depends on the character of the organization.

When you get an organization which is acerbated like the government, for example, then you will get short fuses. The Diet, where a great many people behave like feeding time at the zoo, is a good example of something which is acerbated. But, there too, they're only in there for a couple of years. It's not that long.

The same thing happens in the West too, but the pattern is different and it is usually moralized about, reasons are given. Whether it's the real reasons or not doesn't make any difference.

BK: What about consensus? Isn't that a myth also, in a sense? Is it consensus or manipulation?

DR: Consensus isn't consensus at all. It's brainwashing on the one hand, or coercion on the other; people saying you're going to think this way, you're going to vote this way. It isn't that everybody is sitting around the mystic table being benign and getting the same idea at the same time. It's just the old power play with a few people pushing through what they want to get done.

But here it is done in the packaging technique, as always in Japan.

BK: Tiring people out in a way?

DR: Yes. Or being absolutely adamant—which is considered a virtue, just as being conciliatory is also considered a virtue. A lot of the Japanese now will talk quite openly about this myth. People say that they have never seen this beautiful creature called "consensus". They've attended lots of meetings where there was a lot of bruised feelings, where people were coerced.

BK: Isn't there also a lot of one man shows in this country too? I mean, a company run by one man?

DR: I think that almost everything in this country is a one man show. No matter what their propaganda may say about this, can you really do anything that's successful that's run collectively?

BK: I think the myth is that to get something through you approach people at the middle level; they will carry the proposal up and they carry it down. Even if the president has an idea, he allegedly turns it over to the middle level of his organization to gain the corporate consensus. But in fact hasn't the president really already made up his mind though he may manage people in such a way?

DR: Well, "manage people" that's the operative thing here.

Yes, what you say is quite true. I do believe this, but it is done in such a way that it would also falsify what you're saying. Even though he has made up his mind, you, when he's talking to you, would be the last person in the world to know this. I'm sure that being Japanese and being a person in a position of authority, he would very carefully take his alpenstock and hold it up in front of you and test each step of the way. I'm sure that the knowledge that he had made up his mind never occurs, even though, indeed, he has made up his mind as to what he wants and what he's going to get.

It's the way in which he gets it, the technique. It's the way in which company presidents, or not even them, because more often than not the president will have no power, it'll be the person behind him.

Bislick Kirsten wanted to do a marvellous ballet about power in Japan at the New York City Ballet. He never did it, but it concerned a *shogun*. And then, as in *bunraku* there was another *shogun* controlling him and then more *shoji* would open and there'd be a long chain of people controlling other people, moving their arms and legs, and finally, way in the back, but invisible, there is this little man in Kamakura running the whole thing. I think that is the way things are done here.

Yet, think of the amount of time and care taking in convincing other people, showing them the way and then, of course, getting them to do what you would like to do.

On the other hand, the very fact that you are showing them what you would like to do, given the Japanese feeling for hierarchy, makes it certain that it's done. You do not, indeed, go to someone who is going to get in your way. You don't go to the vice president.

BK: In your own experience with the Japanese, have you ever had an argument?

DR: Not in the good old knock down, drag out American sense, but I've certainly had my fights in Japan. It's been more like guerilla warfare, the snipping, hidden enemy. Then, I've become the hidden enemy. I've become quite good at snipping too.

But given my life, which is mainly literary, I don't have to compete too much and that is one of the reasons I like living here, I don't have to compete. But I have been in situations indeed, where I realized that someone was out to get me and that the only thing to do would be to go out and get them.

I behave then in a very Japanese way. I mean, what you do is you take good positions. I would go to someone I would think was the proper person and not exactly complain about what was going on, but let him know what was happening just for his own information.

If the snipping does not stop, you are then allowed to get other people on your side. Since you're a foreigner, you're really fighting with one hand behind your back, but then, if they are fighting against you, they have one hand behind their back too. It's not a fight anybody's too interested about. Also, if I don't know the rules, then it's no fun to fight me.

BK: Could you describe this in more detail? Could you give an example?

DR: Well, let's see. I got fired once from a publishing house where I had a position because I was not playing their game at all. I had thought I was playing a game where I was confidante to the president and was helping him in his work. I was also helping him by telling him when he was ill advised.

He seemed to take all of this in. He seemed to be acting after talking to me. I was really behaving in what I thought was a responsible way. But, in so doing, I was breaking one taboo after another. For one thing, I was only an employee, no matter how much a favored one. When I would go against his experience of a lifetime, to point out that one did not do this, very often I used ethical reasons: this is cheating, you cannot do this. This is something I see now that I should not have been doing. But I was carried away as most Americans would be, with missionary fervor, making a better person or better world.

Eventually, I did so many bad things, I broke so many taboos, that I found that, while I was still attending meetings, I was being more and more isolated. When I said something, no pencil marks were being made by anyone anymore. Then, eventually, at one time, I was not informed of a meeting.

Then, I would come and find that there wasn't really any work for me to do that day, so, I'd take the afternoon off or do something I wanted to.

It all happened very slowly as though it weren't happening. I see now that it was controlled by absolute fury on the part of these men I had made so angry by not knowing the basic rules of human decency. I didn't read any of this properly. It was years ago. I'd go in and be friendly and the friendliness was always met with smiles, but again I noticed coolness and I noticed distance. But none of this prepared me for what happened.

I had sometime before, when I was still in good favor, put in for a raise and no word was said. All of a sudden, New Year's came, bonuses were received. After New Year's there came a letter, special delivery, from the president of the company. He fired me in no uncertain terms, just like that and gave reasons: I wasn't doing my work, I was taking half days off, I was missing company meetings. Obviously all these things had been arranged. I could not really understand.

The president said he could not tolerate me, was deeply disappointed in me, and so far as a raise goes, well! So, he had the great pleasure of telling me I'd really infuriated him.

BK: He actually told you to stop working or refused the raise?

DR: He fired me, and they don't do that to Japanese. But, then, the Japanese don't do what I did to them. He read everything, from my point of view, wrong, but from his point of view, I did everything wrong. So, this is a fight, and you can see, it'd make a good comic opera!

BK: How did you handle it? In America, you would sue.

DR: Well, I don't come from that period in America. In my period in America, you didn't sue. As it was, I behaved in what turned out to be a rather Japanese fashion. I wrote him a letter, upholding his right to do what he did but certainly deploring the way he did it. There came back a letter saying my severance pay would be this and this and this. It was enormous! Far more than I deserved. I was really getting a golden handshake. Even under the circumstances of not liking me, the golden handshake principle was still going on. Maybe he thought I could have made trouble. Maybe he thought I could've sued, that I would have said something bad. I don't know.

BK: Well, maybe he wanted to protect his own image, didn't want to be known as a person who mistreated someone.

DR: Maybe he did. But, I mean the mistreatment was manifest in the original letter. "You please come tomorrow morning at nine, clear out your desk and be off the premises by twelve" sort of thing. Quite brutal.

BK: That's World War II!

DR: Yes, Pearl Harbor!

BK: Merry Christmas, Mr. Lawrence. Did you see that movie?

DR: Yes. Now, we were talking earlier about this long pattern of holding the fort and grinning and suddenly exploding. This is what happened. I had goaded him into making this decision and I was very surprised. I had not thought such things possible.

How would this have been in America? I would have been given some indication long before the axe fell. But actually, according to the Japanese system, I was given very many. I didn't read their signals, and they misunderstood or didn't read mine.

So, this is a classic example of two acculturated people unable to read the cultural symbols of the other party. This happened to me once. I am much more wary now and much better at reading the signs. This does not make one cynical, just more realistic.

BK: If foreigners are so unreceptive to something they're not used to can they nonetheless contribute to Japanese companies and institutions?

DR: Yes, sure they can. My president was an ex- *kamikaze* pilot. That has something to do with it. There are many company presidents who are going to misinterpret and there are an awful lot of foreigners who are simply not going to cope with it. Nonetheless, they have to try it over and over and over; that's the only hope they can contibute.

BK: Have you had any troublesome experiences in Japan that you might not have encountered elsewhere?

Donald Richie

DR: Nothing that I might not have encountered abroad, certainly. For instance being misinterpreted willfully. Since I write a lot, since I've moved fairly well along in my field, occasionally some smart ass will seek, as indeed it happens in America a lot more than it does here, to grandize himself by pulling down the grand old man for one reason or another. Let's look at Mr. Richie's methodology here, when he hasn't read anything to begin with. This happens with the young Japanese critics occasionally, but not so much. Mainly with would-be intellectual book magazines, but it's scarcely personal. I don't know these people.

BK: What do you think of the standards and quality of criticism in Japan? The newspapers do not seem to have cultivated the kind of critics as, say, the *New York Times* has. I mean first rate people reviewing books and movies and theater. Here it's usually the journalist who is not capable of covering a good police story, broken his arm skiing or something like that. He's told to do movies for the next year. You're dealing with people like that, aren't you? I assume they don't have a critical background, and they probably also belong to factions and being Japanese, may not want to alienate someone, because they're all in the same village. How do you move in that world? You live in the world of the Japanese, but you also live in the world of critics. Don't you also have to deal with the potential ostracization of Japanese organizations, or publishing houses whom you may have offended by not giving their book the kind of review they expected?

DR: The standards as we know in the West certainly abound in private life but they do not exist in public life or in publications. The fact that they don't exist makes life easy in a way. Much of my stuff is translated into Japanese, but the majority is not. Therefore they have no idea of what I'm writing and have no interest in it at all. My being a foreigner writing about the same things they are is again no contest.

It is only when I've been on television or somewhere else where I've forced their attention, then this sort of willfull misinterpretation—it's not ignorance—will come up, but I think mainly it's a childish thing.

Ordinarily, I don't have to fight that battle because I'm not considered an opponent. I'm too different. Again, one of the joys if you're a person like me living in this country, is that you are considered so strange, that any extra amount of strangeness doesn't make any difference.

BK: In the '50s and '60s when you were basically introducing Japanese film overseas—without your introduction some of those books or movies might never have been seen—they must have been sensitive to what you wrote, because you could make or break a name.

DR: That's true, but again, it didn't make any difference to them at that time, because they did not think of film as an exportable item. They had five million people going to see a single movie on a single day here, and they made all the money they wanted.

Money from abroad was gravy. They didn't take film seriously, so they didn't consider that when a foreigner was looking at them internationally. They didn't need the money.

They would get in my way only when I told them how good Ozu was. They'd say, "Look, no foreigner could ever understand Ozu. He's so Japanese". And I'd say "Look, let's send it abroad" and they'd say no, we can't do that. It'll be a waste of money. They sold all of Ozu's movies, he's a great director, and they got good coverage, but they still, to this day, at Shochiku, refuse to believe that foreigners can understand Ozu. It's all a fluke. It's all due to Mr. Richie's exoticism. They will not believe that someone so profoundly Japanese can transcend everything and go directly to hearts all around the world. It's a good example, being absolutely yourself, you can go any place and walk right in.

So, ordinarily, there's been no contest. I have not suffered from that at all. The Japanese who've known about it have always been very good about me. I get prizes and people who know and who love film and who have standards of their own are very pleased with what I did. It's just the opposite of flak.

You were saying earlier that one of the problems was that the Japanese didn't have critics with standards.

I quite agree. When I think about standards, good literary, artistic standards, I always see them in adolescents, kids. Young people. They know exactly what is good, bad, but then when they leave school they're never the same afterwards. I'll see those same kids after ten years with the company and they have become absolutely accomodating, they steer in any direction and where have their standards gone? What's good for the company or what's good for the family or what's good for Japan? You name it.

That's what Mishima grew to dislike in this country so much, it's been endemic here. He particularly disliked what he called the Meiji way. This terrible accomodation, relaxation of all standards. So, he responded by writing *Sun and Steel,* the big standard, you know, and did himself in. The idea of an adult with independant standards—I wonder if it exists?

BK: That may be the weakness of the Japanese system, the group society.

DR: But, is it a weakness? I wonder. If we were going to the Amazonian river culture and looking at a native tribe and realizing that they didn't have any standards except for the good of the tribe, what would we call that? We wouldn't call it a loss, a vice. And, anthropologically, that means the tribe can continue.

BK: That brings us back to the original point. It may all be good for the internal system, but how do you get new ideas and new ways of thinking, how do you deal with the rest of the world if you cannot create new ideas internally?

DR: Yes, yes and that brings us right back to my dilemma too. I've known for years that if Japan got rid of the things I don't like about it, it wouldn't be Japan any more. It'd be something else, Saigon, the Philippines. This is a very large dilemma. It's a real existential dilemma, because by seeking to protect what you have, you will destroy what it is. But isn't this in the larger pattern of what always happens? Isn't this what happens to all tribes, even technological ones like this one? We wouldn't even think of talking about it if it happened to the Navahos, for example, where indeed it did occur.

We are seeing a dinosaur-like structure still surviving here, which is so astonishing, we can't believe it. So, we keep making up reasons for it. We're privileged to have lived inside the dinosaur for the time being, but you know what happens to dinosaurs.

BK: To return to a smaller aspect of this theme, what about creativity in Japan. How creative are the Japanese?

DR: It depends on what you mean. I'm sorry to have to keep passing terms all the time.

BK: I'll give you a vague generality and you can choose what you want out of that. But, if you want to specify, we can talk about technology or about literature. Do they make Broadway-quality musicals? Do they make good movies? Have they written great books?

DR: It's all about imagination that we are talking, right? Let's look at it this way. Imagination is a quality. What happens to the imagination is what we have in the movie or the music or anything else. So, the property of imagination is not so important as what is done with it. So, the answer is, yes. The Japanese imagination is such that it can create these things.

But, if you look at the way the imagination works, in a culture like the American or the West European, originality is one of the high points of excellence and to be original is good. Then you come to Japan and look at the concept of originality and you realize that being original in any way, shape or form is really considered bad. To have your own thoughts is to be hammered down.

In the movies, they like to see the stories they already know, the same scenes, and weep over and over again. Originality is not a concept you would look for in the workings of the Japanese imagination. You have to look at something else then. What is it that it does? Does it reflect the actuality of the Japanese then? Yes, it does. What else about it?

You find that one of the great things about art also occurs in this country and is not hidden: art thrives on art just as science thrives on science. We say the Japanese are copycats, but we're not that original in the West either—at least not as much as we'd like to be because we've got this big myth about originality.

In Japan, people are quite open. You see a beautiful picture, so you go paint it. It's not the same picture. It's different because you painted it. You read a marvellous novel and you think: I want to write a book like that. And you write a book like it but it's not the same one. We find that reprehensible when it is known. Even now, the fact that Shakespeare used other people's stories troubles us. We still ponder about it six hundred years later. So, we've got problems on this, but the point is: the way the imagination works in everybody is that you're inspired by oher people's imaginations and you go out and do something about it. In the West, you hide the maneuvers. Here, you don't at all. You just go and do it. It works no differently than Western imagination, but it does so openly.

If you look at how the radio was invented, you find a lot more than Marconi going on. You'll find anything that you can imagine is done by a committee. I mean the myth of Western originality is really one that deserves to be flung out.

BK: Technologically, what have the Japanese originated? Take the cassette tape recorder, which was developed basically by the US Army in the war, Philips then was the first to patent and commercialize it. Philips still gets around ten cents for each cassette made anywhere in the world, unless their patent has run out. The portable computer or whatever you can think of, it was all there and then improved here.

DR: Or it was made in France and improved in America, or it was made in the Netherlands and improved in Luxemburg. This is going to happen anywhere but it happens so visibly and so much here. Why doesn't Japan do something itself?

Look at the little island with only this many people and compare it to great big countries with many more people working. No wonder they make things for the Japanese to take over. I don't want to be revisionist, and I don't want to be patting the Japanese on collective backs, but it does seem to me that the way they work is no different. Except, that they don't have the myth of originality to believe in and this is a big thing. If you don't have that myth to believe in, how can you be original?

BK: OK. Another theme, the role of women in Japan. Why do Japanese women still have such low status in society? Is it of their own desire, or is it imposed by men who are insecure that women might rob them of their jobs? Aren't they as capable as men?

DR: Of course they are. I've often wondered about that too. Why is it that women are willing to accept men's opinions of them? It must be because a Japanese woman is first a Japanese and second a woman. Both genders tend to think of themselves as first being Japanese and then whatever gender they are. This could be the only answer, why they let themselves so willingly be put on the halters and the blinders. It is telling, I think, that no matter how many women's groups have been started here, they've all come to nothing. It's all ended in nullity. All the members have gone away. They've settled for life seclusion in the *danchi* at the very best. What is it?

It's something very engrained, I suppose, about the Japanese. It certainly goes back to the idea that a woman is not a person until she's married, and then she's not a good person until she's had a son.

These myths have an enormous amount of staying power.

Donald Richie

I've pointed this out as a national pattern. Women start from there; men too. Nowadays they become very Western—Tanizaki, Kawabata, Mishima all went to the West, became very Western in their ways, then there comes a point and they come back and become more Japanese than the Japanese. Wear *kimono* all the time, or do *bonsai*, do something very traditional, indeed. This is true, but what Mishima didn't mention was why: and one of the reasons must be the awful pressure of Japanese society to conform.

Anyway, the role of women has certainly been a successful one from the state's point of view. Women, as you know, are the largest slave force here. Without women to do all those little parts in the transistors, I don't know what the companies would be doing. The working force of women is really very important to the economic welfare of the country. If these women were striking because they wanted to be lawyers or something, or going abroad, then the country would be in trouble.

BK: Who are the Japanese who have impressed you most and why?

DR: This is a very personal choice. Among writers, it would certainly be Nagai Kafu, who is a writer continually dissatisfied with Japan. He went abroad, came back, absolutely dissatisfied. Sort of hated Meiji until Taisho came and then thought Meiji was beautiful because Taisho was so awful. He should have seen Showa! Who behaved consistently as a Japanese, who was absolutely critical of everything that happened and wrote the most marvelous kind of romantic prose about what remained of these stages in Tokyo life. By so being, not only became a great writer, but a social critic. Man of absolute standards.

Ozu Yasujiro, film director, who has imposed on Japanese life through his films a series of patterns, ways of looking at the world, of connecting things which make an absolute transcendant sense, like the *haiku* master at the movies, the tea master. A way of making sense out of the chaos of life, of the formality, which I admire very much.

45

I don't admire any politicians in any country. There are no critics I admire. I admire Kurosawa, the director, because, again, he has a vision which he sets out willy nilly to present. He'll let nothing stand in his way and he'll do so with a great deal of measure. I admire this.

I seem to be admiring people who are denying their Japaneseness. It's not that. I admire people who are using it and thinking about it. Who are aware of it. Usually these people don't know any more about being Japanese than a fish does about water, and yet, they equally depend upon it as the fish does. These people know about it and are able therefore to be constructive about it on the international scale, not just the Japanese scale. I admire this.

BK: How about the businessman, or any individual who's not well known?

DR: Oh, I don't know businessmen; I'm not in business myself. But I know a lot of individuals—my friends! I admire Kuroyanagi Tetsuko, who is a woman and who has made her place in the world absolutely by being herself. I admire it very much when people have a forceful personality and are independent and do this with a kind of dedication to other people, which includes of course giving a lot of money to the unfortunate. But beyond that, when you watch Tetsuko on the tube, she's truly interested in what she's doing, Zen-like. And she listens, she listens a lot. She may have the fastest delivery in showbiz but she also has the best ear. I like that, so I admire her.

We were talking earlier about why people don't get out of their ruts, in whatever country you happen to be in, and why a consensus can so easily enslave a people. I was reading a book about the Morita method of psychotherapy. He was talking about neuroses and it suddenly occurred to me: neuroses can also be perceived on a grand, a larger scale, and a lot of the things that we were talking about in Japan do fit—I have to be careful about how I say this—a description of neuroses. Neurosis is caused by a mechanism which wants you to remain as you are. But when the world around you changes so you can no longer be the way you are and you have to change and your neurosis, which is also your history, won't let you, then you're in trouble.

Japaneseness, in a way, is operating as a neurotic symptom now. The world is demanding this change and yet the ethos of Japaneseness maintains that you have to be exactly as you were. It only wants to protect you, like Mamma. It only wants to be nice to you; it doesn't want to hurt you. This is just the way Japaneseness is working here. You see people going to various lengths to keep all these rigidities here in this society. In the face of what? In the face of change. This is very peculiar because one of the great teachings of Japanese art has been that the world is change. It's like Hiraclitus said. Aesthetic content is when you look in the mirror and see one more grey hair and one more wrinkle, and you look at yourself and smile and nod and say that's the way it is. Time is exactly the way it is.

Japan as We Lived It

"Today Asians do not feel at home here, because the Japanese identify themselves with the West rather than with Asia. That is also why Japan today is not so well liked by Asians."

Japan as We Lived It

Bernard Krisher: Thank you very much, Arifin, for being here with me today. It's nice to have you in Tokyo again.

Arifin Bey: Well the pleasure is mine to be here and meet you again after such a....

BK: Yes, long, long time.

AB: Yes.

BK: This is going to be a wide-ranging interview both to find out a little bit about your experiences in Japan and also about some of your perceptions. Let's start with the experiences, perhaps. When did you first come to Japan and why?

AB: I came to Japan in June 1944, a year after Japan occupied Indonesia and after all our schools had been closed down. I was then at the higher normal school and trying to find a way to complete my studies when I read of an opportunity to do so in Japan. I passed an exam, went through six months of Japanese language courses, and left in April 1944. It took us two months by ship from Singapore to Japan. I remember we were zig zagging all the way trying to avoid submarines. It was a miracle we arrived at all, because almost all ships were sunk midway.

We were housed and taught at the Koku Saigakuyukai in Meguro, which used the building of the American school. There we went through another ten months of Japanese language preparation as well as preparatory courses for the university. In 1945, Tokyo was being bombed almost every day. But nobody thought the war would end so soon, nor that Japan would surrender. I was already twenty. So, when they asked me, where I wanted to go to study, I replied: "I want to become a teacher". There were only two schools of Science and Education then, in Tokyo and in Hiroshima. Because of the bombing they suggested I go to Hiroshima. I got there in April. Four months later when the atomic bomb was dropped, I was right there.

BK: Were you affected at all?

AB: Yes. Very much. I was at school at eight o'clock in the morning on the sixth of August. The reconnaissance planes passed over Hiroshima almost every day at the same exact time—eight o'clock. So we didn't feel there was anything unusual: just reconnaissance, we didn't have to leave the building. In fact, at 8:16 a.m. the all-clear signal was sounded and our professor came to the classroom. Just as he took out his chalk to write down something on the blackboard, there was a flash, a big flash, and everything crumbled over us. Fortunately we were in a wooden building. There were only four of us from Southeast Asia at the school, two in each classroom; all the Japanese students had left for the front.

So, after the big crash, everything crumbled down, everything went dark. We were rather surprised that at eight on a hot, clear midsummer morning, it had suddenly become like evening. Under the debris we continued talking to each other, because none of us was badly hurt. One student said it must have been a big earthquake, so big that we didn't feel it. Another said, perhaps it was a time bomb that had been set up earlier and that now had exploded. Nobody thought of bombardment. It was only two days later that we read in the papers that a special type of bomb had been dropped.

When we could see, we crawled out of the debris and walked for about ten minutes back to the dormitory. On the way we saw collapsed houses and smoke all around. The bomb was dropped at breakfast-time, with most people cooking their meals, on their *shichirin*. The impact of the bomb created a strong wind which blew over all the small cooking fires and in two hours the whole city was burning. Our dormitory also caught fire. Luckily, Hiroshima is a city of rivers and the government had already prepared rafts on the river for just such a calamity. We had just enough time to carry some forty girls, who had been felled by the flash and could not move, down onto the rafts and to get on ourselves to escape. We had put them side by side like sardines, but during the night most of them fell into the water and died.

We survived only because we were still strong enough—

we did not suffer immediate ill-effects of the radiation. The whole school had burned down, so we lived on the campus lawn for about another week, until someone from Tokyo came to fetch us.

Initially we thought we had escaped the radiation illness, but in fact we had been affected. On the way back to Tokyo we stayed one night in Kyoto, where we were warmly welcomed by the foreign students there. We sang and played guitar all evening. We had a merry, merry time. But before morning one of the Hiroshima students, a senior, began to vomit and an hour later died.

On our return to Tokyo we were all taken to St. Luke's Hospital for a check-up. They discovered that my white blood cells had been reduced to 40% the number usually found in a person. The doctor told me he had never treated such a case before and didn't know how to cure me. He said if I signed a form absolving him of all blame should I die he would try to do his best. What he did was to remove the blood from one part of my body and infuse fresh blood in another. So, in effect, I had a full blood transfusion.

This helped. I went through ten years of periodic check-ups and now I feel okay.

BK: How did your parents feel when you left Indonesia? Were they willing to let you go?

AB: I remember my father being very pleased about my being selected because I had qualified through a series of very competitive exams. He said: "It's wartime and maybe we will never meet again, but go because it is for your education". The war and then the Dutch did not permit any communication for years, so we were out of touch until 1952 when I returned to Indonesia.

After the Japanese surrender, I worked for the US occupation forces. There's a saying in Dutch: 'in the land of the blind, one eye is king'. I knew a very limited number of English expressions and I could understand Japanese, so I started as an interpreter and later I landed a job as a translator. This was good experience. When I returned to

Indonesia in 1952 I was able to pass the foreign service exam there and after serving three years in the ministry, was the only Indonesian from a group of eighteen to pass a UN Secretariat test. I went to New York and worked an an announcer at UN headquarters for another three years, using the opportunity to finish college and earn a master's degree.

I returned to the Foreign Office once again, was then appointed assistant director of a newly-founded Science Council and after organizing the first national science congress in Indonesia attracted the attention of the Ford Foundation, which offered me a fellowship for a PhD. I was back in the Foreign Office, when the West Irian campaign occurred (leading to Indonesia's independence) and I thought we needed an English language newspaper to communicate our goals to the world. I thus became the first editor of the *Indonesian Herald*.

I remained editor for six years, until 1965. Following the *gestapu* (the fall of Sukarno after an abortive communist attempted coup d'etat) the Foreign Office needed a different voice, so they named a new editor and assigned me to Japan as counselor for information in the embassy. Because of my knowledge of Japanese, which I had kept up, I was invited to quite a few meetings and symposiums, and I became increasingly attracted to university life.

When I returned to Indonesia, I found myself in an uncomfortable situation. Everyone was stereotyped as either a Sukarno man or not. As a spokeman for the former regime, I was stereotyped. There were no opportunities for me in a responsible position, so I asked once again for an opportunity to return to Japan. A former deputy chief of staff and head of the intelligence service had just established a foundation to compile reports on political security and since they had plenty of money they asked me if I'd like to move back to Japan and send them reports. I agreed because I wanted to come back, and I became the representative of RADA (Research Documentary Analysis). Because of the word 'research' in RADA I received many invitations to speak and landed part-time (*hikojin*) teaching positions at several universities, including ICU and Sophia, before landing a full-time position at Tsukuba, where I stayed for seven years teaching Southeast Asian Studies and Southeast Asian Culture.

But a few years ago I decided I had reached the limit. I became so busy in Japan, I couldn't do anything well. I got perhaps two invitations a week to speak outside the university and I concluded if I stayed much longer people might come to detect that I was a half-baked scholar. Also, my father was getting old and he asked me to come home. At the same time an offer to become vice-rector of a university next to the town where my father lives came along. I thought this was a good opportunity and the best time to leave; that's why I am now in Indonesia.

BK: That's an interesting and unique Japan experience. In fact very few foreigners, if any, whom I know, have had such a multitude of experiences. If you had to sum up very briefly or even in a sentence, what would you say have been the major changes you found between 1944 and 1985 in Japan?

AB: I have encountered four types of Japanese. I call the Japanese of today the "Neoppons". They are not the "Nippons", but the Neoppons—the new Japanese.

When I first arrived in 1944 I encountered, at least theoretically speaking, the spiritual Japanese, who placed more importance on the meaning of life: in man himself, what he is and what he does. What he has, or had, was not very important. To me, coming from a poor country, that kind of Japan was a very attractive Japan. Also, at that time, as Japan was at war with the West, Asia was closest to Japan. In fact Japan had to identify itself with Asia. So we felt at home in Japan during those years.

Today Asians do not feel at home here, because the Japanese identify themselves with the West rather than with Asia. That is also why Japan today is not so well liked by Asians.

Arifin Bey

That was my first impression of the Japanese—self confident. But then I saw the Japanese after defeat. Those were the years of the "empty Japanese". They didn't know what to do, where to go. And they just said: "Let's follow the Americans; we'll do what the Americans tell us". This is the second type of Japanese.

I encountered the third type of Japanese when I returned here as counselor to the embassy. This was the beginning of the era of high growth under the doubling-of-national-income policy of Prime Minister (Hayato) Ikeda. With the expansion of modern highways, built after the 1964 Olympics, and the energence of high-rise buildings, the Japanese also began to abhor spiritual expressions. If you brought up certain phrases which prevailed during the spiritual orientation of Japan, they would say: "don't give that to me".

They began to talk in statistics—how many televisions they had, how many cars, and so on. And they began to compare their way of life with those of Southeast Asians. "If you don't have television in Southeast Asia, then you're underdeveloped..." That was also the start of Japan identifying itself with the GNP of the West and abandoning Asia, so to say. There was an expression in Japanese during the Meiji Restoration, *datsu*, meaning leaving Asia, getting out of Asia. This was the second time Japan left Asia; felt ashamed to be identified with Asia. This was the period when Japan experienced very high economic growth of 10%, even 12% at times; the "economic animal" period.

But in 1972 and 1973 when the oil shock began, Japan came to realize again that she needed Asian friends, because the oil came from Asian countries. Up to then the Japanese regarded Indonesia only as a rubber-, oil- or coffee-producing country, bereft of any cultural heritage or of any religion. After the oil shock, however, they had to rediscover Asian countries and the Middle East. Suddenly they had to know more about our culture, too.

So, after the oil shock I discovered the fourth side of the Japanese. These are the Japanese, who, while maintaining their economic growth have returned to that war-time spirituality and identification with Asia. This is the type of Japanese who begins to talk in terms of culture, in terms of discovering Asia and being friends with Asia.

BK: How do Asian countries, or maybe Indonesia specifically, regard Japan? In a word, how does Japan look from there? Is it regarded with love, hate, envy, ambivalence?

AB: I think we should distinguish three groups: Firstly, those with a vested interest, such as government officials, secondly scholars, and thirdly the common people.

The vested interests, of course, feel that cooperation with Japan means they can stuff their pockets; they can have bank accounts somewhere. You don't get an objective view from them, because they are thinking of their own interests. The scholars are very critical of Japan for the elite in Indonesia is overwhelmingly Western; they think about Japan through the filtered eyes of the West. This is partly also Japan's fault. Japan does not explain itself adequately and that, in turn, is due to the fact that the Japanese are not familiar with the culture of the people they talk to.

BK: You have had a long relationship with Japan, covering many decades and different periods. Have you been able to penetrate right into the heart of the society as though you were Japanese?

AB: Japanese society, you know, is like the Maginot line. You have the core line. You have the middle line and then you have the outer line. They allow foreign influence up to one of these lines. But they never allow any outsider to penetrate into the inner core.

BK: Through the shell, but not beyond the membrane of the egg?

AB: Exactly. They are very deceptive. Congenial only up to a certain extent. They emasculate their language, for example; allow foreign words to penetrate. But when it comes to the inner core of the Japanese value system, you cannot touch this; it's "We Japanese." For example, at the outer level, they always say "We World Peace," "We World

Community". When they're outside their country, they talk in terms of internationalism. But once they're back home it's "We Japanese" again. And this progresses further in small circles: "We Mitsubishi", "We Sumitomo". And within this core they have further cores.

Thus, you may be able to penetrate Japanese society at large, you may get involved, but you never penetrate into the core. A foreigner may become an advisor of Mitsubishi, but not a real official member of Mitsubishi. They give you high names, even good pay, but no *real* involvement or permanence.

BK: What personal experience have you had in this respect?

AB: Well, when Prime Minister (Zenko) Suzuki went to Southeast Asia in 1981 he said in a speech in Bangkok, that the time had come for the Japanese and ASEAN people to cooperatively work and think together to realize common objectives. Inspired by his words, I gathered a few friends in Tokyo and proposed the establishment of an ASEAN society. We established such a society here with a membership of Japanese and ASEAN-countries' citizens. We asked a member of Parliament to become the chairman, we had two Japanese vice-chairmen and I became the ASEAN-side vice-chairman. This organization was very small. We held monthly lecture meetings and we published a newsletter. One of the vice-chairmen of the Japanese side then suggested we register the society as an incorporated body with the *Gaimusho*. That would made us eligible for some financial help as we were, after all, also promoting the policy of the *Gaimusho*.

The *Gaimusho* was very polite during several discussion meetings. But nothing moved for more than a year. Finally someone whispered into my ear that "unless you resign as a member of the board, our organization won't be recognized, as no foreigner is allowed to be a member of the board of a body which is financially assisted by the *Gaimusho*". Now remember this association was established through contributions of pocket money. I myself invested about 500,000 yen in order to get it moving. A few Southeast Asian friends also invested. I was flabbergasted. Here you have a prime minister talking about "let's work together and think together." And then when an ASEAN society, the kind of organization he himself had proposed, was established with only one foreign member who speaks Japanese on the board, then I'm told the Foreign Office says "no foreigners".

BK: And what happened?

AB: I resigned. And I think the society got the *Gaimsho's* approval.

BK: Will they be effective?

AB: I don't know. Now it's totally a Japanese show. When I checked with other "international" associations, I found it was the same. Even the UNESCO association which in many other countries is a mixed nationality affair, is exclusively a Japanese affair here. That's the point: when you come to the core it has to be kept pure.

BK: Can Japan survive forever with such an attitude? Isn't the rest of the world going to react in kind someday? Can Japan continue forever to enjoy the best of both worlds?

AB: So far they have managed to do it. To the Japanese, their Japaneseness is more important. Multi-racialness is the American way of survival—the Japanese survive through purity.

BK: On the other hand, is it all that comfortable to be in the inner core? I, for one, would much prefer to be excluded from some things and therefore not, in return, be forced into so many obligations. After all, isn't Japanese society quite suffocating for the Japanese? You must always be on your guard to be polite, not to confront, you owe so many obligations. You can't let your guard down and ever really be yourself. For someone like myself it would be a life of quiet desperation.

AB: That is true. You can't have it both ways. Once you are admitted you have to conform to their rules.

However, there is another way of getting in; namely,

keeping a distance but still be in. On many occasions, I have been the only foreigner invited to various functions. Yet, once I recognized that the discussion was not to be heard by a foreigner, I voluntarily got out because when you stay and something is decided then you belong to it and you have to abide by it. So you have to know how to play the game. In such cases I didn't feel excluded. In this sense I penetrated just enough and yet kept my freedom of maneuver.

BK: What about the Japanese academic world? How does it differ from that in the West, or Indonesia? Is it also a repository for ideas?

AB: Here again I have to talk in circles.

They have places for only certain types of academics. I know, because I have participated in committees where participants for conferences or symposia are chosen. When I proposed we invite a certain professor known to hold certain unique ideas, the response usually was based on whether he belonged to the type and if he didn't they would invariably say: "let's see where he fits later". This meant, of course, he doesn't fit in this program. In other words, they always look for people who express the same kinds of ideas as others. A conference or symposium in Japan looks for harmony and consensus. Safe ideas. Nothing that resembles debate or confrontation.

I've been thinking about this more deeply. My own interpretation is that in the West, or at least in cultures with monotheistic religions, the pattern is to arrive at the truth through a confrontation of ideas. There is also the Greek tradition of dialogue, of asking questions repeatedly until the answer comes. Such a tradition is alien to Japan, where, instead, the big *sensei*, a Confucianist type, tells his apprentices that things should be managed in the following ways; one, two, three, four, five. The apprentice will then memorize this. Thus knowledge in Japan, as they learned it from China, is a conveyor belt. The teacher dispenses wisdom; the student receives. There is no dialogue, let alone debate. If you ever attended classes in Japan, you would know that the professor comes in and says: today we begin with page so and so, and he would then read from his paper or from his book. And when the time comes he says, "now, that's all for today," and he would walk out.

BK: Is there no interplay between the professor and the students?

AB: None. The student cannot debate. Sometimes they don't even ask questions. "Say, *sensei*, I read quite a different view in one of the books I bought, what do you think about it?" You would never hear a question like that in a Japanese class.

BK: How would a Japanese professor react if a student actually began to debate him publicly in the class?

AB: To begin with there would be no time for it. The professor talks from the beginning to the end and he winds up by stating, "that's all for today." And even if a student were to raise a question, the professor would respond with: "why don't you come to my office in five or ten minutes?" After that the student would lose his courage.

In my view, the Japanese student obtains knowledge only until he graduates from high school. When he goes on to college it's just a playground or a moratorium, so to say, before starting on his career. At college the criteria is to attend classes and one gets good marks by remaining in the good graces of his professor. Even getting into the "right" university doesn't prove all that much. There is an art of passing the test, you see; it is not so much what you know but how you have mastered the gimmicks of taking the test, which you can learn in preparatory school.

BK: Do you have any theory as to why the Japanese are so energetic and work so hard while Southeast Asians put much less effort into their work. Is it cultural, climatic or some other factor?

AB: Originally, of course climate played an important role. You can see that even by looking at the Japanese in Indonesia—they don't work as hard there as they do here in Japan. Another factor is that accomplishment is held in very high respect here; you are respected if you work hard and people listen to you.

BK: But why are Indonesians also not so entrepreneurially oriented? What is it in the culture that makes people almost shy away from accumulating wealth or becoming successful? Sure, there's a certain class of people in Indonesia, but mostly of Chinese origin, who are motivated to work for material benefits, but among two hundred million Indonesians why are there so few who aim to work hard and build up big fortunes? Is it due to the luxury of being surrounded by such a wealth of natural resources?

AB: Part of it of course is the climate. The second is the spiritual, cultural tradition; while Christianity commends people who work hard, other religions favor a more aesthetic way of life. Hinduism and Buddhism for example; they preach that the less you spend on materialistic things, the happier you will be. You know, Buddha began his teaching by discarding his wealth and his possessions. And while Islam doesn't actually urge its adherents to live in poverty, they do urge their followers not to overdo it: not to waste, but enjoy what is available. With such a philosophy the followers tend to shy away from any extravagance, even to feel ashamed if they are better off than others. There's another social phenomenon that discourages people from getting rich. And that's the fact that the successful member of any extended family is expected to care for all his relatives. This pressure to share property with the family causes many people to feel that success is too great a burden to carry.

BK: What experiences have you had which you can draw on to discuss the quality of friendship among and with the Japanese?

AB: In all the time I lived in Japan I think I had the most friends during the oil shock; even people I didn't know, who happened to be in the oil business, sought me out and implored me—because I come from an oil-producing country—to say that Indonesia should not join the oil boycott against Japan. Japan was initially categorized among the countries considered to be enemies of the Arab world and there was the fear that Indonesia, an Islamic country, might think similarly.

So, not just one or two but so many businessmen suddenly called on me and invited me to dinner. But as soon as the oil crisis subsided, these people disappeared; they never called me again.

BK: Is there anything the world can learn from Japan? Is there anything you'd like to see Indonesia, for example, adapt from Japan?

AB: There's no such thing as a general principle that could be adapted universally. But in the case of Indonesia I would like us to adapt Japan's meticulousness to detail, as opposed to our culture of "approximate."

In Indonesia, if you ask someone how much they earn, they will say: *about* 400,000 yen, instead of the exact amount. Or if you ask: "What time are you coming tomorrow?" They will reply: *"around* nine o'clock." Also, if you buy stamps at the post office and you're supposed to get 20 cents in return, the Indonesian clerk will not return it and the customer won't demand it, because you are not supposed to pay attention to such minor details.

But here in Japan, and also in the States, you are right to get and expect even one cent back. I would also like to have Indonesians appreciate the aesthetic values. I would like more of them to visit Japan, not to study, but just to walk and see how the Japanese keep things clean—the streets in front of their houses, the sign boards, everything, including the toilets, are meticulously clean.

BK: Another area that is often debated is whether the Japanese are creative or imitative. What do you think?

AB: If you define creativity as beginning from zero, then they are not. If creativity also includes beginning from one, then they are perhaps the best. If they see something, then the idea comes to work and they say, from this I can make this and refine it to this, and further improve it to this. But it's still difficult for them to create something from nothing; at least at present. Perhaps they will be able to, in the future.

BK: In other words, they didn't invent the computer, but they may be the first to come up with the fifth generation computer. Finally, I know you have already returned to Indonesia, but, after spending a total of twenty-one years in Japan, didn't you ever give any thought to spending the rest of your life here?

AB: Not really. Apart from wanting to return to the country of my birthplace, I also concluded that you can only be happy in Japan as long as you are productive; you are only welcome here, as long as Japan profits from your existence. When the time comes when your contribution lessens and approaches zero, no one wants you. This is not a society where a man of old age could enjoy himself. Even the Japanese old-aged don't enjoy themselves, let alone the foreigner who is going to be an added burden to society.

BK: Do you have any regrets then, that you stayed twenty-one years in Japan? Was it a wasted effort or the wrong place to be?

AB: No. I think it was the luckiest part of my life because I learned so many things. I witnessed a vanquished nation walk up the ladder and become one of the major countries in the world in a matter of less than thrity years. I learned the value of recording history. The respect for knowledge and realized Japan is perhaps the only country in the world that honors its most creative, talented people by naming them National Treasurers.

BK: We talked before about the closed Japanese society. Did you ever consider that has been an advantage to you, after all?

AB: Yes, when I think of. It reinforces identity as an Indonesian. If I had lived in America that long, I might have been absorbed in the melting pot. I agree with you, I think I'm more of a nationalist today because I stayed so long in Japan. You can only be happy in Japan as long as you are productive; you are only welcome here as long as Japan profits from your existence. Knowledge in Japan, as they learned it from China, is a conveyor belt. The teacher dispenses wisdom; the student receives. There is no dialogue, let alone debate. To the Japanese, their Japaneseness is more important. Multi-racialness is the American way of survival—the Japanese survive through purity.

"The Japanese press has an astonishing ability to self-discipline itself."

Japan as We Lived It

Bernard Krisher: John, you've been with the Associated Press for forty-seven years, in Japan for the past twenty-five; you're the dean of American correspondents. You're seventy years old and retiring this year. Let's start at the beginning.

John Roderick: I started with the AP in Maine in 1936, the year after I graduated from college. I worked there for six years, then went to Washington, then got involved with the Army. I was in the Army for three and a half years, ending up in China with the OSS. When the war ended, I sat down and sent a telegram to Kent Cooper, then the general manager of Associated Press, and told him I'd like to rejoin AP in Japan, because in the interim I had studied Japanese at Yale, and I told him I knew the history and the background. He said, "Right. Join AP in China." I've always suspected he didn't know much about geography. When the Communists took over I had to leave China and eventually got my wish to be assigned in Japan after some years in the Middle East and Europe.

BK: If you could relive your journalistic career, would you have preferred to have worked elsewhere?

JR: I don't think so. I never felt the problems, particularly in Europe—Paris and London—were very germane to the struggle of living that you see in Asia. In London, I was reporting on politics, on Churchill's rise to power or return to power. In Paris, I was writing about Rita Hayworth's marriage. I was involved in lots of things that didn't really seem very important.

In Asia, however, I always felt very strongly that by being here and by reporting on the poverty, the misery, the struggle for human existence, particularly in the Third World countries of Asia, that I could, in a tiny way, contribute to help ease that. For me, that was the main reason I wanted to stay in Asia and in Japan. Although Japan is obviously not a Third World country, it started off that way in a sense and the problems here have been somehow far more related to the human condition.

66

John Roderick

BK: What has been the story in Japan that has interested you most?

JR: My career in Japan has been kind of a split one. I started off, as I told you, in China. I loved China and I also spent six months in the caves of Yenan, the Chinese Communist capital, where I interviewed and got to know Mao and Chou En-lai. I was so involved in China and I wanted to keep involved. I first became the AP China-watcher in Hong Kong. Then I moved to Tokyo finally and we moved the China-watching function of the AP to Tokyo, because I was there. So, my career in Japan has been divided between covering China from Japan and covering Japan from Japan.

BK: Then let me ask you this: China is the mother of Japanese culture and yet the Japanese have mixed feelings about China. On the one hand, the Japanese recognize China's influence on their language, their history, their culture; on the other, they see themselves as a superior technological entity vis-a-vis China; what are the differences between the two people?

JR: That's a very good, complex question. They're vastly different, as you know. The Chinese, perhaps because they are a continental, not insular, people are more straightforward, easier to understand than the Japanese. Continents seem to breed philosophy and introspective thinking; their populations look out at the broad range of subjects that can interest men and women.

Japan had taken many things from China but adapted them to its own needs. So, what you see in Japan today, say art, bears a resemblance to the Chinese and uses Chinese themes in, say, the *imari* or the scrolls; nonetheless, it is purely, totally Japanese. The Japanese put their imprint on a work of art or even in a way of doing things that the Chinese don't, that Americans don't.

BK: Which of the two societies do you prefer?

JR: Of course, I prefer Japanese society today, because I've lived here for twenty-five years. I haven't lived in China during that time nor would I want to live in present-

67

day China because it's an authoritarian, Communist society. Although I love the people, I admire them, under no circumstances would I ever think of living in Peking or Shanghai, as I did think I would have wanted to, before the Communists took over.

BK: Do you think the Japanese would be different if they had more space, if they were not an island country? Is the lack of space a major determinant of the Japanese character?

JR: Yes, it certainly is one of the major determinants. They're an insular people, very much like the British in that sense. People laugh at the Japanese organizing their own little societies when they go abroad but they forget that the British dressed for dinner and had their own style, kept very much to themselves and hardly mingled at all with natives when they lived in Africa or India. And you didn't find the British intermarrying with the Asians. The French did, the Dutch did and many other colonial, imperial countries did, but not the British and not the Japanese. That is because of their insular mentality and a kind of "pure" race pride.

BK: Speaking of the British and the Japanese, there are many similarities, but Britain, in recent years, seems to have moved away from this. The British royal family today is an interesting royal family compared to Japan's imperial family, and the Beatles also came out of the British. The British nurtured a great many new phenomena that the Japanese don't seem able to do.

JR: That's true. The reason is that Japan is on the edge of a civilization, the Chinese, which is not scientific. Although gunpowder and the compass were invented in China, that was long ago; there has been very little scientific progress for the past two hundred or three hundred years. On the other hand, England has been on the edge of a very productive continent which has had all the great scientists, and, as a result, produced creative people of its own these last few centuries. China's cultural contribution to Japan stopped a couple of hundred years ago, whereas it's been a different process in Europe. Britain profited from the industrial and scientific contributions of Italy, France, Germany, and turned out some first class people of its own. I think that's the difference.

BK: Moving to the subject of reporting from Japan, how do you, as a journalist, assess the difference in news coverage between the Japanese and the US press? Is this a more difficult society in which to ferret out facts, to contact people? Is Japan a closed society? How did you get your information?

JR: There's no question that it's much easier, much more comfortable to cover news out of Washington than Tokyo. Washington has a highly developed press relations corps which the government uses. The government is used to having daily contact with the press and trying to get its message across to them. It has been said that the Washington press corps is spoon-fed; you don't hardly have to lift a finger.

But in Japan reporting is entirely up to the correspondent. Nobody hands out anything in Japan. Your press briefings often don't produce much information; rather, lots of evasions. Of course, that's true of Washington and London and Paris, too. Nonetheless, one doesn't feel one is getting the straightforward information here. But, if you go to a source that you know in a ministry or office, it doesn't take too much effort to get the story. People in Japan are not unwilling to talk; it's just that they only want to talk to friends. They will not talk to the public, or to a press man just because he's a press man. In fact, they may even withdraw. But, if you get a man privately, you have a drink with him, you know him, then you'll get a lot of information.

BK: Where do you think the public is better informed, in America or Japan?

JR: In any given political situation nobody's very well informed. What you get, you have to dig out. If you just relied on the ordinary sort of transactions of government and politicians every day, the world would be totally misinformed. It is totally misinformed as it is, but it depends on the journalist himself to be able to work hard and correlate facts to be able to get a story and the right story. That's why in America, as a revulsion against this spoon-feeding, we've set up investigatory teams. AP has one, the *New York Times*, various other organizations have them, and their job is to go to Washington on a given story, on things you wouldn't otherwise ordinarily hear about.

BK: That brings me to the next point. Japan and the United States are perhaps the two most interesting working democracies in the world today and they operate on distinctly different principles. In the United States we pursue a confrontational democracy; here in Japan we see more of a consensus democracy. The role of the press, we agree, is basically that of a Socratic gadfly, the media are supposed to make the politicians uncomfortable by scrutinizing their every act and thus serving the interests of the public. Which of the two, the Japanese or American press, if one can make the comparison, serves democracy or the public better?

JR: I've almost become Asian enough to favor consensus politics, compromise; you accomplish more in the long run with that kind of a political system. Confrontational politics is very abrasive and often doesn't reach a conclusion at all. You just argue with each other. However, where the press is concerned, confrontational writing is far more useful. A lot of stories are dug up in America which make headlines because a reporter dug up the facts. The classic case is Nixon and Watergate. It's almost inconceivable that Japanese reporters would have dug up Watergate. The closest they came to was the Tanaka affair, and, as we all know, that started off in a magazine and it wasn't picked up by anybody until the Foreign Correspondents Club put Tanaka on the griddle. Then the Japanese press was able to go ahead and pick up the story.

Today, the Japanese press is becoming more aware and doing more than they used to do, but, I'm afraid, they are still inclined to follow the government's lead too often. Two examples: One is the case of coverage of China. It was a scandal back in 1971, when Lin Biao defected and escaped to Mongolia. His plane crashed and he was killed. That story was not reported for months in the Japanese press. And yet, the Japanese press corps was fully represented in Peking. Why? Because they made an agreement before they went to Peking not to report anything which might be detrimental to the relationship between Japan and China. I don't know why they considered this would be detrimental but they decided so and they didn't report it.

The second case was the coverage of the Cultural Revolution. The Japanese press played a very important role as far as the world press was concerned because those Japanese who were based in Peking went down to Democracy Wall every day in the middle of the winter and, with frozen fingers, took down everything that was on it and very accurately reflected what was going on in China. We in Tokyo caught this. Their reports were the basis of some of my best stories. I picked them up and sent them to America where they produced big headlines. One day, Chou En-lai got annoyed with all this and called the Japanese press in and said, "No more. I don't want you to do this anymore." They stopped.

Now, to me, that was an abdication of their responsibility. These are two examples, and you know, there's even a third example: the visit by Korean President Chun Doo Hwan to Japan. A good will trip. A trip that I think personally was all to the good. Anything that will bring together these two old antagonists is a positive thing. But the press of Japan appeared almost sycophantic in never mentioning his background or about the society he rode over. They called nobody's attention to the fact that Korea is such an authoritarian society. If it were really a free press, they could have done it; somebody, at least, could have.

BK: How do you account for it? Is this self-discipline, built-in national interest, or is Japan, in a sense, a subliminal, totalitarian society?

Japan as We Lived It

JR: I don't think the last but, it's sometimes the consequence of consensus. We know the press clubs, the *kisha* clubs, often control the mood in the sense that they will not report on certain matters. They decide amongst themselves that this is not something worth reporting or we're not going to report it. We had this example during the Vietnam war. A South Vietnamese vice premier or ambassador would give a press conference in Tokyo. Nobody would be there except the foreign press. Not a single Japanese would show up to report on what he said. So, it never appeared in any of the newspapers. The Japanese press has an astonishing ability to self-discipline itself in that sense, but by doing so, they do their readers an injustice.

BK: How does it effect the strength of Japan's democratic foundation? Is Japan capable of withstanding a serious crisis, and still remain democratic?

JR: Yes. Funnily enough, I think Japan would withstand a crisis and remain democratic. Not due to the confrontational concept of press versus government, but perhaps because of the opposite. Japan is a Confucian society. The strength of Japan lies in its sense of belonging, working together as a family. It's obvious you can't have democracy in a family. If the youngest stands up and tells his father to go to hell, he's going to get knocked down. It won't work. But in America, it does. So, there are democracies and democracies. At the same time, Japan is a leading democracy. You can do almost anything you want within reason here. I can think of almost no country on earth where you have Japan's freedom of speech, freedom of assembly. You have demonstrations every day; the freedom to express yourself, almost too much. I don't know how in the case of crisis Japan would react, but I think it would not come apart.

BK: If someone were to ask you how have you changed by having lived in Japan, would you be able to distinguish some differences in your personality, your character, your way of doing things? Has this society had an influence on you? You mentioned one thing before that you

believed in consensus politics. Would you have believed in
that had you remained in Washington?

JR: Yes, that definitely is something that has influ-
enced me.

When I was living in America and in Europe too, I was
very much in favor of confrontational politics. I felt interplay in the marketplace was very important. I've since
noticed how destructive that can be and I wonder really if it's
the answer. Living in a country like this has definitely
affected me. It also certainly affected my eating habits. I've
discovered an entirely new cuisine. I love *sushi* and *sashimi*
and *sukiyaki* and all the rest of the Japanese cuisine, which
is one of the most underrated cuisines in the world. It's so
varied all you have to do is go through the food section of a
department store and see the hundreds of different ingredients and foods, and you realize it's not just a simple cuisine
at all. That's just one area.

But I've also grown a little bit intolerant in Japan of
some attitudes and customs. I do love the Japanese, otherwise I wouldn't have stayed here for twenty-five years, but
there are periods when I actually hate some aspects of Japan
and I'll tell you what these are.

One is the so-called family suicides. They're not
suicides at all. Usually, the mother or the father murders
their children and then commits suicide. I find this appalling. Why do the Japanese do this? Why doesn't the press and
why doesn't society try to create an atmosphere, a mould
which condemns this?

I know the basic reasoning: when a mother or father is
despairing and they want to kill themselves, they fear to
leave their children alone; they'll be alone in the world,
orphans and that would be a dreadful thing.

Well, this is not so today. It was so during the Edo Jidai,
because orphans actually had a very tough time. They
perhaps didn't survive. But today, you have countless examples of orphans who have risen to very high positions in
business and government, all over. It's unnecessary and

cruel and terrible that parents who love their children should choose, should be so selfish as to do things like that.

Another area which has upset me considerably is family structure. It is deadening to see parents, particularly the mother, exerting such a powerful influence on her children's lives. As Ian Buruma points out in his book, *The Japanese Mirror* in a chapter titled "The Eternal Mother," the Japanese mother scrimps and saves during the early years when her children are small to put them through the best schools, so that they will have the opportunity to make something of themselves after they graduate. We all know that syndrome of schools in Japan. She may even undergo physical hardship in the process of saving money to do this.

All right. It's a great debt, a marvellous thing, something to be admired. But, then she starts calling in her debts after the boy or the girl, usually the boy, has graduated from university and wants to choose a bride and an occupation. She and the father, but mostly she, decide almost always. If they don't agree, there's usually hell to pay, great traumas.

BK: Or they take it out on the daughter-in-law?

JR: They take it out on the daughter-in-law. The mother-in-law wants to be waited on hand and foot and wants the husband to be waited on hand and foot. It's a very feudalistic hangover, to the discredit of Japan. It is also a blow to feminism. It's women depriving other women of their equal rights.

Now, fortunately, the dispersion of the families to the big cities has changed a lot of that and many families are now not living with their parents as they used to. They have their own separate apartments or home. On the other hand, these feudal ties are renewed every year at *Shogatsu* (New Year's) and *Obon*. They go back to the countryside and they get the message again. It's there and it's quite extraordinary. These two aspects of Japanese life don't go with the industrial, aggressive capitalist society it is today. In other words, Japan still has one foot in the feudal past and one foot in the twentyfirst century.

74

BK: Except for the mistake of the war and the consequences it paid, which has probably benefited her in the long run, Japan has done fairly well for herself. Does Japan still possess the correct formula for future success? Or, must she make some adjustments in order to deal with the problems facing her in a rapidly changing environment? Is she equipped to deal with the pressures caused by her trade surplus, her low defense expenditures, the growing threat of terrorism?

JR: Japan is singularly badly equipped to deal with the rest of the world because of her insular position and because of the feeling among many Japanese that once they're educated abroad or once they become experts in a subject, they know it all. Consequently, there is an unwillingness to learn from other societies except about technological aspects and the things that will do them immediate good. This may be true of many societies but more so in Japan and so Japan has got to change. It has got to come to grips with the rest of the world. This unwillingness to get involved deeply in international affairs is one of the great Japanese weaknesses. A case in point is the lack of participation by Japanese in such international organizations as the UN. Yes they join the UN, the IMF, etc. but very few Japanese serve in those institutions.

BK: Internally, then, what makes Japan function so well? Is it because of its homogeneity, that everyone thinks alike? In that respect, has the American 'melting pot' really worked?

JR: Yes. I definitely believe the melting pot has worked. The activity we get from so many races coming together in America, even the confrontations we've had, release immense energies. After the fighting is over, everybody's ready to knuckle down to work. We've had bad times, we've had the inequities, the injustices, we've had labor problems, we've had robber barons, but, basically, the society survives. There's a considerable freedom in it. I don't know if you could have that same kind of freedom in

Japan on the same basis because we come from a Christian-Judeo background, basically. We've operated this way for centuries and we are comfortable with it. It's the opposite in Japan, however. Japan comes from a Confucian, Buddhist, Shinto background and they couldn't operate outside that context. It would do injury to the social fabric if you tried to change it.

BK: Which society is better in toto?

JR: I don't think you can say that one society is better than the other. All you can say is one may be better adjusted than another. Japanese are more comfortable with their government and culture. Americans are also comfortable with theirs. Attempts to try and impose one on the other are always disastrous, and this has been an American fault. We've always tried to impose our culture, not only on Japan, but, particularly, in China, and there's where we really lost out. We've rarely been willing to adjust to the ideas of others.

Take religion, for example. The Catholic religion attempted to make converts in both places. They succeeded rather well in the beginning. In both countries they had hundreds of thousands of converts. The Jesuits were even willing to go a step further and take on some of the trappings of Buddhism and even of Shinto, some of the rituals and the costumes. But Rome decided against it. Theirs was the great heresy. It was the thing that broke the Jesuits and had them outlawed for a number of years. This offers a classic example of how the West, particularly in religion, was unable or unwilling to adjust to the East. And how many Christians do you have in either of these countries today?

BK: Do you consider the Japanese a religious people? What do they fall back on when they're desperate or tense?

JR: There are Japanese who are rather deeply religious. You can see it in the countryside where people follow the religious festivals, go to the shrines and temples and follow in marriage and birth and death all the rituals thereto. They don't go because they're forced to, or they don't go to see their neighbours, as we do in America sometimes, or to show off their best clothes. They go because it is a thing they must do and it's part of the Confucian heritage as well.

Although they are religious it probably doesn't completely satisfy their emotional stresses to the extent that it ought to. There are people in this society who are under heavy emotional pressure and don't know how to get rid of it. There is a lack of psychiatrists. The number of alientated people in Japan is shockingly high and nobody seems to know what to do about it. They seem to try to cover it up and keep it at home, or dismiss it as a passing thing.

It's one of the main problems in Japan amongst the old, and it's going to get worse as the parents get older and their children are married off and live in another area. When they retire, they don't know what to do with themselves. They've worked so hard all their lives, their full raison d'etre has been scrimping and saving and working hard from morning to night to keep life together and put their children through school. And, suddenly, one day, they're not wanted. They're not doing the job they were doing and they've nothing to do. So, unless they can travel or they have some interests like reading or playing golf, they're going to be lost. In the countryside it is the most serious. It often ends up that they have become mentally unstable or they make life miserable for their children and their families. This is one of the major problems of Japanese aging.

BK: You are ending your association with AP and you are retiring at age seventy this month. Why have you chosen to stay in Japan, rather than go back to Maine or somewhere else in the United States?

JR: Well, I may eventually do so. I'm not sure. But having spent twenty-five years of my life here—it's a very big chunk of my life—I feel very comfortable in Japan. I have a Japanese family, an adopted son and his wife and their families who are very close to me and I like them. Indeed, I love them. Then, in addition to that, I happen to live in an old Japanese farm house in Kamakura.

BK: Tell me a little more about that.

JR: I acquired the farmhouse eighteen years ago through Yotchan, my adopted son. One morning at breakfast, in Kamakura in a rented house we lived at, I brought up the subject to him. I said "I've been living twenty years overseas as a foreign correspondent and spent thousands of dollars on rent with nothing to show for it. I would really like to have a house of my own." I said that the money that newspaper correspondents get is little and I have very little money to build a house with. In fact, my budget was $20,000, but, anyway, it would be nice if I could ever do it.

He didn't say anything but a couple of months later he said why don't we go to a village up in Fukui prefecture and take a look at it. He said there were old Japanese farm houses up there, one of which I might be able to buy. I said, well, I still think it's impossible considering the price of land and everything, but I was glad to look at it.

So, I went and saw this old farm house built by the old Heike descendants, deep in the mountains. It was a charming house with big beams and pillars and a thatch roof and I really fell in love with it. So, I asked the Japanese farmer who owned it how much he would want for it and he said 5,000 yen. So, I took it.

Well, it was so cheap because they were building a dam in that area and the villages were to be flooded, so he had to take the house down, and Yotchan and his family persuaded him that I would be someone who would care for it and look after the house. In effect, they gave it to me. I stored it for two years, because I didn't have any land and it took two years to find the proper piece of land. I found it in Kamakura on a hill, high up on a hill with a very nice view, and I bought it, again, for a song. It was nothing. My whole expenditure for the house and land at that time was $20,000, and it is now a show place. My son has gone into the antique business and he has a house next door to mine, also a 250-year-old Japanese farm house. Well, we've had many interesting people visit us, including Vice President George

Bush who came when he was Ambassador to Peking; also Ambassador Mike Mansfield has been here, and the wife of Vladimir Horowitz, a number of people in the theatre, motion picture and literary world, and Walter Cronkite.

BK: What was your most disappointing or unhappiest experience in Japan?

JR: Actually, my most disappointing experience didn't happen in Japan but it was while I lived in Japan. It happened in New York City in 1971 after I'd gone to China with the American ping-pong team. I was one of only three American correspondents to go, and, as Chou En-lai, the prime minister, had said, "Mr. Roderick, you open the door," at that time I had become suddenly something of a small celebrity. It seemed rather natural to me that when Richard Nixon would be going to China the following year I would be assigned to cover that story but when I asked my then general manager, a fellow named Wes Gallagher, whether I would be going on the trip as one of the three-member AP team he said, "No, John. You've been there" and he didn't send me. That was the most disappointing moment in my career. I was on the verge of resigning from AP and maybe even quitting Japan. It was personally a great disappointment but it's hard for me to think of a disappointing moment in Japan with the Japanese. I've lived a kind of charmed life in Japan.

BK: What is the most striking change you've noted in Japan during the time you've been here?

JR: The most striking change is physical. Since 1963, the year before the Olympic Games in Tokyo, as we all know, Japan took off like a rocket and the construction boom that took place not only affected Tokyo but spread to most of the country.

When I first got here Tokyo was a collection of little villages—twenty-three wards and each one was almost like a country area. No big buildings because of the danger of earthquakes. One felt really as though one was in the countryside, only there were more people and you had all those charming little alleyways, paper lanterns and lots of little *yakitori* bars and stand bars. It was a delightful sort of place.

I once heard that you could not take a major city, like New York City, and rebuild it or rennovate it but I think this has been successfully done with Tokyo. I dare say, it is really a beautiful city. That area around the Imperial Palace, the moat area, is one of the most beautiful areas in the world, when you think of cities. And walking down that road past Police Headquarters toward the Ginza, at night particularly, it's very striking.

BK: What could we learn from the Japanese and what could they learn from us?

JR: The single most important thing we could learn from the Japanese is arriving at decisions through consensus. What we should not learn from the Japanese is to be so insular. I think that is something they could unlearn from us; they should immerse themselves more and more in Western society.

BK: Who are some Japanese who have impressed you?

JR: Former Prime Minister Hayato Ikeda impressed me immensely, particularly as a human being. He was a deeply religious man. He told us once when he was in despair he had made the arduous pilgrimmage to the Buddhist shrines and subsequently recovered from an illness.

He also impressed me immensely because he approached a relationship between the United States and Japan, which was at an ebb, if you remember, after the fall of Kishi, and he did it with a low posture, which was exactly the right thing to do at the time. He was a man willing to compromise with the Socialists and even with the Communists and he was in favor of consensus, whereas Kishi had been confrontational. Kishi's approach was a prime example of how confrontational politics don't work in Japan. Kishi tried to ram through the Security Treaty and look what happened. Japan came to the brink of great confusion as a result. Then Ikeda came along and, in conjunction with Ed

80

Reischauer, who also had the same laid-back ideas, was able to help Japan really put its feet back on the road.

In the literary field two people have impressed me immensely. One is Kawabata—I knew him before he received the Nobel Prize. The other is his disciple, Mishima. I got to know Mishima fairly well personally. To me, he was one of the most extraordinary Japanese in this period, because, again, he illustrated the possibility of having one foot in the feudal past, the other in the present. He yearned for the old days of the samurai, of the way of the warrior, and, at the same time, he was as modern as he could possibly be. He was a brilliant writer, a brilliant conversationalist, a person who was delightful to be with personally. If he came into a room and sat down, he'd be the life of the party; very outgoing. I never thought he would do what he did. There was a sort of quirk in his mentality that was very curious.

I don't know how to explain it. I don't know whether it exists today very much at all except in the extreme right wing people, but he was neither left wing nor right wing. I don't know what he was doing. He was perhaps just an exhibitionist but he was impressive. He could have turned out at least a dozen more books of his experiences but he got so caught up in this whole business of the feudal past, in the loss of principles, how the emperor had been debased. He didn't like all these things. They worked to create in him some kind of a complex plus his desire for the theatrical sort of exit from life.

BK: In winding up, what would you like to conclude about yourself and Japan?

JR: I chose to spend twenty-five years in Japan and I've come near the end of that experience. One would think that one would look back with regrets and say perhaps I should have been somewhere else, perhaps I should have done something else. But I can't honestly say that. I feel that it's been worthwhile being among the Japanese people. But, of course, one also has to put into that equation the fact that I was doing an interesting job and that professionally I was kept busy. And I got paid for it and I travelled. I was able to go around Asia as well as Japan at someone else's expense. It was all very interesting and delightful.

James C. Abegglen

"There is too much emphasis on the mystique of Japan."

83

Japan as We Lived It

Bernard Krisher: When did you first come to Japan and how did you happen to come here?

James Abegglen: It was a long time ago. I first came to Japan on October 1945 as a member of what was called the Strategic Bombing Survey. I was 17 and studying at the University of Chicago but was afraid the war would end before I could get into it, so I volunteered for the Marines and at the end of boot camp; I selected to go to radio school but instead was assigned to Japanese language school to be trained as an interpreter who would interrogate prisoners of war. When I got to Guadalcanal, however, I was told the unit didn't take any prisoners and they made me a scout. I was subsequently wounded at Iwo Jima and recuperated in a hospital. Then we were pulled back into Honolulu for some special training preparatory to the Kyushu Invasion. The first landing in Japan was to be in southern Kyushu and our division was to be the assault division. That invasion, fortunately, never occurred.

When the war ended, I was twenty and in rather bad shape. But I wanted to see Japan and so arranged to get myself detached from the Marines to the Army. That brought me to Japan, to Hiroshima, in fact, for about six months. I had wanted to stay in Japan but my orders stipulated a discharge in the US so I returned to university intending to continue studying Japanese. However, one of my professors persuaded me to begin in another specialty and then focus on Japan later. I took that advice and went off to a Ph. D in social sciences. And then I went back into Japan studies in the fifties.

I have often reflected and I certainly have no answer short of thorough-going, in-depth psychoanalysis as to why I became so intrigued by Japan. I suppose part of it could be attributed to my combat experience. People who are in direct combat generally burn out whatever hostilities they may have had by the experience. It was interesting. Several of us who had been for this long period in the South Pacific found ourselves in Japan, in that brief period when we were very young, much more sympathetic to the Japanese than to the Americans. We were thin and gaunt, beat up, and so were they. The Americans we met were amply dressed and amply fleshed out. No doubt some of it was a very complex identification process in which we leaned much more toward the Japanese than the Americans.

BK: What was your background in the States? Did you come from a big city?

JA: Oh no, no, no. Tiny, tiny village with a population of a hundred and six way back in upper Wisconsin. A dairy community, unpaved roads, one church, three saloons and a blacksmith's shop. Tom Sawyer, Huck Finn country.

BK: Was there no other alternative, perhaps; was it either going back to that village or staying in Japan?

JA: No. When my father, who had had a cheese factory, died, we moved to a slightly larger city in order to attend better schools. I became, rather, a typically midwestern fellow who, typically, became fairly upwardly-mobile and would follow that mobility channel through the university and out into the big cities.

BK: How did you come back to Japan?

JA: Most of my studies were in clinical psychology and I wrote my doctoral thesis at the University of Chicago on the personality of upwardly-mobile businessmen. I then applied for a Ford grant to do a comparative study of US and Japanese factory organization. I then spent a year at Harvard preparing for my study by pursuing sociology and anthropology courses, and, mainly by doing Japanese studies under Ed Reischauer. A terrible course, and then I came back out here in 1955 for about a year and half.

The hypothesis of my study was that since the countries are fundamentally different and the cultural history different, then the social structure of the factory must also be different—and I wanted to study this. Yet, at Harverd, where presumably the top experts on Japan were, no one could tell me whether I could get into a Japanese company to study social structure. No one had ever done it. Quite literally, nobody had ever taken the trouble to study a Japanese company. Sounds a little bizarre now in 1980s, but, in 1954, no one knew whether the management of a Japanese company would be willing to be interviewed or whether you could visit their factories.

When I arrived in Japan in the summer of '55, I went first to try to enroll in some seminars on industrial psychology, I was refused by a distinguished professor, who explained: "my students don't want foreigners in the seminar". He added, however, "If you will get some money, I'll work with you on a repeat of your research in America". Well, I found that a fairly appalling response and, with that, avoided Japanese universities ever after.

I fortunately had a letter of introduction from the then head of ITT to the head of a Japanese electric company. That letter was the entré that worked. It opened the first door and then others. "Now, here is this rather naive American who has studied a little Japanese and has done some management consulting in America but is basically a scholar and wants to find out about Japanese companies", they thought. They were fascinated and so the hospitality and assistance was simply superb. Looking back, it's almost unbelievable. I was so fortunate, so lucky. These people were so hospitable. For example, at NEC, the man that I was, in a sense, turned over to was Kobayashi Koji, who is now chairman and the man rated by middle management in Japan as the businessman they most admire and respect.

Then, by separate introductions, I went to Toray, Fuji Steel, Sumitomo. That all led, rather by chance, after another year or two to my book, *Japanese Factories*, published in '58. I had expected it would be of modest interest to American scholars but of no interest at all to the Japanese. It turned out to be of modest interest to American scholars, who reacted that, "this can't be true because companies can't work that way". But it was a raging best-seller here and it gave me a peculiar position in Japan because I was seen as having special insights.

James C. Abegglen

The book hit Japan in the mid-fifties recovery, as the country began to move to the high-growth era. Up to then they had been preoccupied with importing Western technology and Western management methods. What I was saying, in effect was: look, don't import Western personnel methods or you'll screw your system up. It was a very powerful message from a Western expert, to tell them: "don't try to copy the US system of compensation, job evaluation or recruitment; it's not going to work for you". It was a message that they were ready to hear—which, I'm sure, is one of the reasons why that book and the things associated with it, have had a rather long life in business and intellectual circles.

BK: Then you got into a career of consulting in Japan. How did that start?

JA: No. Actually, I went back again to the US and became a professor at MIT. I was unable to support a family on their salary, however, so I jumped ship, joined ITT and came back to Japan in 1957 with ITT, spending a lot of time also in Saigon, Bangkok, Taipei as kind of an area person.

I went back to New York with ITT but found my personality and the headquarters style of such a large company didn't really fit terribly well. So, I moved to consulting with Arthur D. Little. Spent three years there. But, in the process, I found myself spending more and more time in Western Europe and less and less time with Japan. So, in 1962, when McKenzie & Company, asked me to join them and help them think about Japan, I left ADL and moved to McKenzie.

But in the mid-sixties when McKenzie subsequently decided not to open an office in Japan at that time, I left them too, and joined what has since become the Boston Consulting Group.

BK: I know consultants don't talk much about what they do but what could you tell me about your activities over the past fifteen years?

JA: Our work, during that period, from 1967 to 1974,

87

was essentially and entirely devoted to foreign companies interested in Japan. Most of it was entry.

BK: The problems faced by an American company entering Japan reflect, in a historical sense, the larger US-Japan problems of the era. In retrospect, what can be said about missed opportunities?

JA: The problem through much of that period, and this is still the case, was that most companies in the West were not prepared to spend the time and resources and effort to do in Japan what it would be in their long term interest to do. The frustration of a consultant arises from seeing opportunities and offering a way of dealing with them and not being able to get people to pick up on it.

BK: It seems many American companies have had much less resistance to entering a new market, say, in Europe or elsewhere in the US. In what way was Japan so different?

JA: Well, one of the ways in which Japan is different is it is perceived as being different; more remote, more unique, more difficult. Americans in Europe had more of a sense of being at home than in Japan. And of course, through much of that period— at least until the early 1970s—Japanese government regulations themselves were also a great barrier. You couldn't freely invest here until the early '70s. Furthermore, Japan is an extremely competitive place. Entry is not easy and good personnel are difficult to obtain. Entering Western Europe was possible without undue problems, such as acquiring a Western European company and using that as the vehicle for expanding. In Japan, companies are not available for acquisition—at least until recently they haven't been—not because of any laws but because of the nature of the company in Japan. And so the whole mode of entry into Japan was essentially barred.

The combination of earlier government regulations, really very keen competition, high land prices, and the difficulty of hiring management staff, create a fairly formidable obstacle. However, those companies who were determined, whose senior management, for whatever reason, reached an absolute conviction that "by God we're going to be in Japan whatever it takes because it is so important both as an opportunity and so important as a potential competitive threat," those companies—like Texas Instruments, IBM, AMP or any number of other companies—they are in Japan and they've done very well and it's been very, very valuable for them.

BK: What is wrong then with American companies? Why are so many opportunities being missed? Is it the structure of decision-making in the United States? What are the basic problems?

JA: I think it's terribly complex. I don't imagine that we could settle it, although there is a presidential commission looking at it. One problem, of course, although it applies more to some products than others, is the exchange rate. A continuation of the present rate distortion threatens to gut American industry. If you take the distortion to be say 30%, that means that a US company selling in the world markets has a 30% barrier in addition to whatever tariffs there might be. And it also means that the Japanese company selling in the United States has this 30% subsidy. Well, there are very few people, given a 30% subsidy, who are going to fail to sell and there are equally very few people, given a 30% barrier, who can manage to sell. In addition, there is a whole range of other problems.

If you look at autos, or a solid company like Caterpillar competing against Komatsu, you see the American companies are dealing with the UAW. Here we have an instance of monopoly in labor prices.

BK: Actually, your knowledge is so vast and the topic is so broad, maybe in an interview of this type we should try and narrow this to several substantial examples. Can you cite some case histories thich might illustrate such points as the difficulty of getting into Japan, having the right product for Japan, selling in Japan or finding good people to work for you?

JA: Let's take one field in which the Japanese have not yet made any significant impact in the United States—air conditioning. Now, in large air conditioning, the Japanese won't be a major factor in the world because their own market for very large air conditioning is quite small; they can't get the scale advantages of cost. But in smaller air conditioning, the kind that would go into a window or into a small house or into a small shop, let's say under five ton sizes, here the Japanese now have a cost advantage over the Americans who are the principal players in the world.

In every single export market, the Americans are losing their share or the Japanese are gaining a share, and that's been going on for several years now. So far, in air conditioning, the Japanese are not yet significant players in North America but they clearly are going to be there. Daikin just landed in Miami a few months ago, Mitsubishi Electric and Toshiba are setting up franchise arrangements with dealers in California. You can see the game they are starting to play. It's a game that's been played out in many other industries.

What does the American air conditioning industry do? They are in real danger of having a technological as well as a cost disadvantage because the Japanese are working on technologies in air conditioning that aren't available in the United States. You really need a fairly bold move. And it seems to me the bold move in this case would be for an American company to join with a Japanese company in production of the key component of an air conditioner, the compressor, in Japan initially, and perhaps fairly soon afterward in North America.

In the process, you would get the Japanese technology. You would give the Japanese a participation in the US market but you would retain position in the final product and that would be a strategy that would both recognize the strength of the Japanese and protect the position of the Americans—in fact, eventually give the Americans a renewed advantage. It takes a degree of courage because the problem hasn't arrived yet. But you're going to have that problem two or three years from now.

A factor which causes some American companies to push such problems aside is this: Let's say you're sixty one or sixty two years old, you're president of a company and your retirement pay depends on profitability for the next two or three years. Then, this problem is somebody else's problem. It's easy to put it off. That kind of thing can often be an issue, disturbingly.

So, here is another industry where the American players of the game are not going to react to a clear impending threat fast enough, although you would think with Detroit's example and Xerox's example and all the other examples that they would be inclined to move very fast and hard, and yet they are not doing it.

BK: Isn't it ironic that in Japan the directors and the chief executive officers who have a much longer period of control and much fewer perks and benefits somehow manage to make wiser decisions than in America where some CEOs are paid close to seven figures sometimes?

JA: Well, of course you don't want to say this of all US chief executives. Also you must remember that they are living inside the biggest market in the world; other markets tend not to look that important. The CEO will say: don't bother me about Japan, for heaven's sake, Peoria is burning down, or: I've got a big crisis in Jacksonville, or something of the sort. The US market is so huge; it's still twenty to twenty-five percent of world GNP; it's enormous. And more than half of the generation of people who are leading American companies grew up in the period where America was literally half of the world economy. It's perhaps unreasonable to expect men whose entire training was in that environment to become suddenly very sophisticated about the fact that America is no longer half but is only twenty to twenty five percent, and that Japan is no longer two percent but is now ten percent.

It may take another generation of people, much more

internationally-minded, to begin to think more in world terms.

BK: Give me a success story.

JA: Take Nestle, which has well over a billion dollars in sales in Japan. The last time I looked, Japan alone accounted for fifteen percent of Nestle's worldwide after-tax income. It's an incredibly profitable business, essentially all coming from instant coffee—they have something on the order of seventy percent of the market. They have been here for a long time and they worked very carefully not to try to change or revolutionize the Japanese distribution system, but rather to work within and adopt to it by using detailed teams, supporting their wholesalers, working through trading companies, taking advantage of the system and, consequently, reaping enormous success. I remember that in 1960 their market-share and that of General Foods was about the same, and Morinaga was also a major factor. Yet, in that famous Japanese consumer market, which is supposed to be so difficult to get into and to be successful in, they pushed these competitors aside.

The key was distribution. One of the things they did was to work through the trading companies, giving them a commission. On the one hand, you had all those layers of distribution that would ensure proper stocking of all the retail outlets. At the same time, they dispatched their own teams of salesmen out into the retail stores to help the retailer arrange the stock and shelves, crediting the sales to the wholesaler working to pull things through the system.

General Foods, meanwhile, failed by setting up an American style sales force which went out and did direct selling: trying to change the system instead of working through it.

BK: Nestle was never tempted to short-circuit the mutli-tiered Japanese distribution system, to eliminate all these intermediaries and distribute directly themselves?

JA: Well, the chain of distribution has been shortened of course in most areas but, remember, if you're Nestle you have to sell at least 750,000 outlets; those tiny little shops don't have any credit, they don't have any warehouse space. When the owner of such a tiny shop down an alley somewhere needs six cans of instant coffee, some little boy gets on a bicycle and brings it. He doesn't have credit, he doesn't have inventory space, he needs an instant reaction. No big company can react that way; you've got to use that wholesaler system if you're going to cover Japan nationally in that fashion.

Coca Cola is another example of a totally different product which also worked through Japanese companies. When you talk about Coca Cola marketing, you note first that Coca Cola has only twelve or fourteen customers in Japan.

BK: A tangential question before I ask you for another case history: Coca Cola or IBM are examples of successful American companies in this market. What if they set up their own trading companies to handle other American products, would this be a good way to penetrate the Japanese market?

JA: A lot of people have looked at that possibility. One reason it may not have been done is that no one really wants to make Coke richer. This, I think, is probably the basic problem and yet, on the face of it, I think the generalization I'd make in the consumer area and certainly in the food industry is that the companies which have done well in Japan have done so through the distribution system of the Japanese.

If I have only a single product or very few products and I'm trying to get them through an extremely costly distribution system, I'm simply not going to make it. I really have to ride on the back of a Japanese company's distribution, whether I'm Nestle through the trading companies, Coke through the bottlers, or Nabisco through Yamazahi and CPC through Ajinomoto.

BK: What about joint ventures? Some Americans have hesitated moving in here on their own but have opted rather to enter through a joint venture.

Is that the preferable way?

JA: The joint venture is a curious phenomenon. The joint venture has almost always been an unsatisfactory compromise of conflicting interests: the American or European company sees the joint venture as a beachhead into Japan while the Japanese see it as a way to secure technology: a fundamental incompability of objectives. Furthermore, joint ventures have usually been between companies in the same industry, which means those companies are ultimately going to come into worldwide conflict.

So, it isn't surprising that in the last few years even very successful joint ventures have seen one side or the other taking over the ownership position.

For example, Dow Corning, a very powerful company in silicone chemistry, has had a very successful joint venture with Shenet Chemical and Metallic Silicone. There was an agreement, as they are competing worldwide, that one side or the other would buy out, and Dow Corning sold its position. It also had a very successful venture with Toray in liquid silicones and, in this case, Toray sold out, giving Dow Corning the controlling position. International Harvester needed money and sold out its half of a very succssful venture to Komatsu. Hewlett Packard has just taken 75% of what had previously been a joint venture with Yokugama. TRW took almost the entire ownership of a joint venture they have had here. Dow Chemical and Asahi Chemical had a huge chemical venture and they split—Dow took part, Asahi bought part and they are now separate companies.

A joint venture implies a degree of congruence of objectives that's unlikely to be sustained for a long time even if one is successful. One of the great exceptions, however, is the Fuji-Xerox venture. From the Fuji film side, they wouldn't have been in copiers, presumably, if they hadn't formed a joint venture with Xerox. And Xerox has pretty well left its hands off the venture, letting the Fuji side run it. The fact is that the Fuji-Xerox joint venture is probably more successful than Xerox itself is.

But the era of the joint venture being the dominant bold type of foreign investment in Japan is over. Companies coming in now will either set up their own operation directly or do something different. You've now got this breakthrough, represented by Merch's acquistion of Banyu, where it looks as though it will be increasingly possible for foreign companies to buy a significant position in a Japanese company. They will not be the leading Japanese companies, they'll be companies that have some problems, but it will at least be a way of entering this market. Because, if you acquire a successful, ongoing company in a highly developed market, you already have staff, facilities, distribution, government relations and positive cash flow from the first day.

The alternative, so far, has been to buy land, terribly expensive and hard to get; find staff, terribly hard to find; set up distribution facilities and get the distribution channels started. It means at best you're going to have five to seven years of enormous negative cash flow. You can avoid this with an acquisition.

In Europe—Britain, France, Germany—typically about twenty percent of the activity in the economy is in the hands of foreign investors. In Canada it's more like sixty percent and Australia it's thirty. In the US, it's probably something on the order of six or seven percent and in Japan it's less than three percent. In my view, the inability to acquire Japanee companies is largely what has reduced foreign investment here. That, of course, arises from the nature of the Japanese company, where the concept of buying and selling people as you buy and sell businesses is regarded as immoral.

BK: What mistakes have foreign companies made in regard to dealing with their Japanese employees?

JA: Typically, there are two things they do badly. First, in interviewing candidates for employment, the qualities Western businessmen would find attractive—a certain ease and casualness, openness, good English—are, on the whole, qualities that the Japanese put a rather negative value on. These are qualities that are going to make an employee relatively ineffective.

The other is the impatience, if you will, of American or European managers wanting to promote by merit; that plays hell in a Japanese organization. It's perfectly acceptable to give a very able chap in a Japanese organization a good deal more authority and confidence; to give him formal title prematurely is, however, very dangerous, because you can't get the title back.

The biggest problem for the foreign company here is its inability to initially attract outstanding people; you are taking the best you can get. But, as you get bigger and more successful, you now are able to begin attracting distinctly better Japanese. And that creates a problem because the fellows in your organization who are more senior and therefore in higher positions are distinctly less able than the fellows you've been hiring for the last few years with less experience but whom you daren't appoint. This situation is extremely widespread among foreign companies here. But there isn't a damm thing you can do about it. You just have to wait.

Yet one of the startling moves in recent years in Tokyo was IBM's decision to move two hundred foreign families into Japan.

Many years ago IBM had its Asia-Pacific headquarters in Tokyo. They layered it on top of the local company and then argued that their local company was purely Japanese and had no foreigners in it. The fact is they took that layer off and thus had a company here in Japan, a huge $2 billion company which was essentially all Japanese-staffed. Now they have suddenly reversed direction completely. It's interesting to speculate: clearly IBM was losing it's share in Japan, clearly they perceived at the top that Japan was critical to their future both competitively and as an opportunity, and, suddenly, at immense cost, they moved people in here who can't be very effective.

James C. Abegglen

Put a foreigner in Japan and, no matter how clever he is, he's not going to be very productive the first year or two. Particularly for a company which has made almost a point of pride of not having foreigners here, it's an extraordinary turn.

BK: Why did they do it?

JA: I don't know why, so I can only speculate. I think what happens with Japanese in a foreign company is that, regardless of their ability or creativity, they must also learn to accommodate to a strange and rather difficult environment, that of a different language and a different pattern of response.

My sense of it is that IBM just wanted to have a very high impact in Japan and shake it, shake it hard. Just shake it up. I can't believe they had any illusion that these two hundred families here are going to be very management-effective for this period that they're here. I think they just wanted to hit the local organization and rock it off balance and jar it away. There is a sense of Big Daddy here. This is how the company does it and you defer.

BK: Had something happened to the local organization? Had they lost their market share?

JA: Well, Fujitsu passed them in the computer market, which got a lot of attention in Japan, and, I suppose, in Armonk as well. They also needed to put a PC into the market here and had to go OEM to Matsushita to get it, which was a new move. They wanted a leasing company and they set one up with Orient Lease and Morgan. I understand it was done over the head of and against the strong views of the local management here. I think they felt they needed more new departures and strategies in dealing with Japan and that they weren't getting that from the local organization.

BK: Was this the correct approach?

JA: It was a calculated risk. They couldn't see any other way of impacting the local organization quickly and felt there was an urgent need to shakeup. There is a joke: The president of IBM Japan, Shiina, was quoted as saying, "What we are going to have now in Japan is the horsepower of the Japanese and the planning ability of the Americans," and someone countered: "I hope they don't get the horsepower of the Americans and the planning of the Japanese."

BK: Let's say you had real international power. How would you reduce the multi-billion dollar US trade deficit?

JA: The focus ought to be on restoring the exchange rate. Without effective action on getting the dollar-yen exchange rate right, you really can't do anything; so, the only ultimate answer is the exchange rate. And, as the US is running massive deficits, I don't see how the exchange rate can really be fixed. If and when it changes, it can be very costly to the United States, yet very necessary, and that will change the trade balance.

However, one of the problems, let's face it, is that governments do not trade, companies trade. One of the difficulties we have currently is the US and Western European governments saying loudly and repeatedly: Japan is closed. To the extent they continue to say that and are believed by their constituencies, no one is going to try to get into Japan. And by not trying, they prove that it's closed. You set in circle a self-fulfilling prophecy.

Now, leaving out the exchange rate, which is a whole other issue, the single most valuable thing would be for Secretary of theTreasury Regan and others to lower their voices and start urging US companies to make efforts in Japan commensurate with Japan's importance. They should be encouraged further by offering some tax relief. An investment in Japan should be compensated by allowing the investor to expense it in an accelerated schedule, permitting one to capitalize it. There are various ways in which you could make it more attractive for US companies to make a genuine effort to be in this market.

BK: What American industries would benefit from this?

JA: Those that export anything that has energy in it:

petrochemicals, chemical fertilizers, paper and pulp, all non-ferous metals; the whole raw materials processing sector where Japan is at a substantial disadvantage and where the United States enjoys lower electricity and raw materials costs.

But one would have to let the market decide that; you can't call these things. Nobody is out there saying you can't sell. You have to work at it. Nobody in the United States invites the Japanese in, they also had to work at it. The issue is to get the companies to make the necessary efforts to be here.

BK: What about consumer products? If someone came to you with a consumer product that was doing quite well in the States and wanted to enter Japan, what advice would you give?

JA: Well, you have to be careful and look at the market very closely. But, take Wella, the German cosmetics company, one of the largest in the world, privately-owned: they came into Japan in the 1970s practically from scratch and are now the largest factor in the hair-care market in Japan, an enormous success.

BK: How did they do it?

JA: They came in here on their own and spent the necessary, money. Furthermore, they spotted a weakness in the market and used a very clever approach. They first moved into the professional shops, using the beauty parlor/salon as a staging area, if you will, and then into the consumer market. They've also been very clever in dealing with wholesalers, getting close to the wholesalers' family, getting their wives involved, sending their kids to Germany. The fact is they identified a product opportunity and did what was necessary by way of investment of time and advertising. This is what I meant by the danger of the US government saying the market is closed.

BK: What type of person should be based here to represent a foreign company?

JA: It's quite important to select the right person. You

can immediately think of some obvious problems. People with teenage children have trouble integrating into the city because Tokyo is rather difficult for the foreign teenager. So, you probably want either a youngish couple whose kids are still in elementary school or an older couple whose kids are off in college.

Wives are also under greater stress in Tokyo than their husbands: he has friends, associations and activities that go with the job while she's often left at loose ends which can be very stressing to the marriage relationship. So, you also need a couple where there is a good deal of resilience and adaptability, which is a function of intelligence. The key is to get some very bright people either quite young or people whose kids are off at college. The family is the key because a guy can be destroyed if the family can't respond to a crisis.

BK: What about longevity. How long should an executive be posted in Japan?

JA: I think five years is probably about the optimal period. Three years is too short because you don't have enough time to make use of what you've learned, yet if you get much past five years, you lose political and cultural touch with the parent organization and begin to have difficulties as a result of becoming more and more isolated.

BK: Many recent books have been written about Japan—Japan, the superpower; Japan, the fragile blossom and some contend Japan is a conspiracy. Do you want to dispel any of these myths or create some of your own?

JA: I am collaborating on a book right now on the *kaisha* the Japanese company, in this case the Japanese competitor, and we want to be at some pains to present it neither in terms of a miracle nor in terms of a conspiracy, but with a calm voice, try to describe what it is that explains Japanese competitive behavior. For the most part Japanese companies compete as they do because of the environment they've been brought up in which is one of high growth, of fierce investment competition and fierce price competition.

James C. Abegglen

Starting from about 1978 or 1979, we have reached the midst of a major change in the basis of competition with Japan.

The Japanese competitive position was built primarily, initially, on cost, and then on quality. Within the next ten years we're going to be competing with the Japanese on innovation and research. The effort Japanese companies are now putting into research is extraordinary. As a proportion of their revenues, it is substantially greater now than that of American companies and that's a big change. It portends a change in the very basis of competition with the Japanese. It's no more going to be a price competition or quality competition only, it's going to move toward innovation and technology competition.

Another myth to be dispelled is that Japan is a monolith; Japan has winners and losers. It has companies that do very well and companies that do very badly. There are industries which do well and those which do badly. We don't hear too much about the losers abroad. There is that danger of portraying the Japanese as being all-successfull, all- winning. That's nonsense.

BK: What is the biggest flaw in this stream of books that come out about Japan?

JA: Too much is made of the cultural peculiarities of those things somehow presumed to be unique to Japan and not enough of just straight economic analysis. The Japanese havn't repealed any economic laws. They respond to the same basic macro- and micro- economic laws everyone else does and they are dealing with the same kinds of environment. There is too much emphasis on the mystique. Whether it's the mystique of Japan Incorporated or the mystique of harmony.

BK: What about the work ethic; is it declining?

JA: After the war, you had a famine in Japan, inflation had destroyed whatever financial base there was, the cities were destroyed.

I don't think it's surprising in that context—with unemployment high—that the system of career employment and seniority pay, which maximized security, developed.

Now, let's take younger Japanese. Today, as many Japanese own their own home as do Americans. The Japanese family has considerably more money in its bank account than the American family; it can save more. There hasn't been any significant unemployment in Japan since the early '50s; forty percent of the kids are college-graduated, when it used to be only one percent. These kids surely do not have anything like the same concern with security as did their parents, nor should they; they are much more likely to opt for higher opportunity risk. They'll take a chance on a job and if it doesn't work, they'll try something else or even try to set up their own company. Those things are likely to be perceived by the earlier generation as a decline in the work ethic, as less sincere, profligate behavior. But, in fact, it's a very natural consequence of greater affluence and more power.

On the other hand, if you check *The Economist*, which runs those statistics every week, in only one economy in the world have hours worked per person gone up since 1975: Japan! Even if one were to argue that the work ethic is declining, so is ours, and it's declining at the same rate, and the gap is staying the same!

BK: Getting back to you personally, what has kept you on here in Japan all these years and what are your future plans?

JA: Well, I've lived in New York, Paris, Mexico City, Chicago, a lot of different places, and I've been, I think, in every major city in the world for extended periods.

I find Tokyo now the most pleasant and interesting big city in the world. Tokyo is a city that steadily improves. Most cities are deteriorating, almost visibly, as you watch. London, for example. Tokyo is becoming a little greener; the air, a little cleaner; the houses, a little nicer; and the streets, a little better. Also, Tokyo works. The cops do a good job, the water runs, the fires get put out.

James C. Abegglen

Tokyo is safe. All that has a high value. Also, I like the way the Japanese work and play; they work hard, they're well-trained, they take work seriously. And, when they play, they play hard. I happen to feel comfortable in that pattern.

And, on the whole, I find a high degree of civility in Japan. The shopkeeper smiles when you go in, thanks you when you leave, even if you didn't buy anything; the clerk at the counter doesn't bark at you, or try to ignore you. People prefer, on the whole, to be polite rather than rude. In the States, on the whole, people prefer being rude.

BK: Which society is better then, American or Japanese?

JA: I think you'd have to say by most measures of social health — infant mortality, life expectancy, level of education, level of literacy, etc,— Japanese society is now a healthier society than American society. It is even perhaps improving: longevity is extending, educational levels continue to rise. It's a very strong society.

BK: Are there any Japanese you particularly admire?

JA: I suppose, in a funny kind of way, Hideyoshi. He certainly did some unattractive things, like the invasion of Korea, but he came up a long, long way in a fairly short time, in a very turbulent, late sixteenth century Japanese society, and moved very, very far to unify this country. He was a man of no physical attractiveness, and certainly a man of none of the inborn advantages.

BK: And from contemporary Japan: business leaders or politicians?

JA: Well, I have an enormous regard for this chap Kohayashi of NEC, a man who was not only able to keep both his human values and corporate vision at a high level simultaneously, but also able to demonstrate a very high level of intellectual performance. I also admire a great many of the Japanese literary figures—Tanizaki in particula. Also Soseki—but not Mishima.

BK: Are there any Japanese you don't like or have you had any disappointing experiences with any Japanese?

JA: Well, probably many foreigners have had the experience of meeting a Japanese, or a Japanese couple, with whom you have had really a very warm interaction that you feel very good about. You have every expectation to get together, and then they simply vanish and are never to be heard from again. Which is to say, then, that a lot of what the Westerner had read into the interaction really wasn't there. This is the frustration of being the outsider.

BK: Have you seen yourself change, in any way, by the fact that you've lived in Japan all these years?

JA: I don't see it, but I'm told there are differences, I'm told, for example, that my voice changes in timbre and that I sound a good deal more pleasant and less threatening when I shift from English to Japanese.

BK: Have you learned anything from the Japanese in dealing with people?

JA: Yes, maybe in taking more time, being more careful about imposing a solution; trying to develop patience, giving time and space for people to work out their solutions.

BK: Do you intend to live here forever?

JA: Well, forever is a long time. But certainly as I look out, I'd be quite comfortable here. Let's put it this way: There's only one country in the world that has a national holiday called Respect for the Aged Day, and I am living in it. And I'm getting old.

"Look, boys, here's a very powerful country, and there's a lot to learn from them."

Japan as We Lived It

Bernard Krisher: How did you get connected with Japan?

Ezra Vogel: I came rather late. I was a graduate student in sociology and in psychology in the Department of Social Relations at Harvard and I was studying for my thesis: families of emotionally disturbed children and families of normal children. I was interested in the relation between sociology and mental health. One of the teachers at that time was a young fellow named Bill Caudill who studied anthropology and mental health. He had just got back from Japan and, among other things, he asked me if I would go over some of his data.

As I was finishing my thesis another one of my teachers, Florence Cluckhorm, said to me "You know, young man, you've never been out of the United States, you're very provincial; the Department of American Social Sciences is far too provincial. If you want to get any perspective on your society and understand it, you have to get overseas. Before you settle down and as soon as you get your Ph.D, please go overseas. And if you don't go overseas, I won't write a recommendation for you." She was partly joking but she really wanted me to go overseas and my wife and I also wanted to go overseas. Since one of my instructors, Caudill, had some Japanese contacts, he said if I wanted to go to Japan he would be glad to make some introductions. One of the people he introduced me to, by the way, found a house for us right next door to him and that's where we rented the first year in Japan. That person was Takeo Doi.

BK: Really!

EV: This was long before either of us were famous so when we get together we joke that we knew each other way before either of us had any notion that either of us would become famous. We had many interesting hours of discussion; it was a completely Japanese neighborhood and we learned from Takeo Doi an awful lot about Japanese society and people, and my wife became very good friends with Takeo's wife. So that was our beginning.

Ezra Vogel

BK: What year was that?

EV: That was 1958. I came here under a two-year grant from the Foundation's Fund for Research in Psychiatry. The grant was to cover one year of language studies and one year of interviewing and research. My plan was to interview families with normal children and then also do families with emotionally disturbed children.

BK: What did you learn about American society from that initial experience in Japan?

EV: Well, like many people who come to a new country like Japan, I first of all learned how American I was in a lot of things. I thought I was a rational, sensible adult. I realized many of my attitudes, about individualism, honesty, and openness were really very strong. I thought that Western society was so far ahead in almost every way—not only economically, but socially and politically—that our democracy was much more advanced. I felt our academic work was at a much higher level; that the Japanese were derivative, by and large.

I guess, though, that a great many things I learned about America in Japan didn't hit me right away. But it hit me later on. One of those was on returning to Japan after a while, I began to notice those extraordinary changes and it made me realize, how slow America was in adapting to those changes. I'm still thinking, you know, about America and still getting new perspectives today. It's a constant revelation, in a way.

BK: In the area of mental health, did you find any differences between the two countries? Is there a difference in the way the Japanese perceive mental illness, and the way they treat it? What constitutes abnormal behavior and normal behavior in Japan?

EV: I concluded normal and abnormal was really very similar in Japan and in the United States so I decided not to write that up because I didn't think it was all that interesting.

Therefore I didn't really spend a lot of time with my original problem. I was much more interested in just describing Japanese family patterns which I wrote up as my first book—The Japanese Middle Class.

But about mental health—there was very little recognition of the mental health problem at that time. It was the period of concentration on economic growth and new technology. The basics, such as personal adjustment seemed of secondary importance at the time, much like consumer products which had to come later. I was doing a lot of cross-cultural reading on mental health and came upon the "town fool" pattern which you find in many developing countries. That is, before you have large mental hospitals in a society, the local villages have their own way of dealing with abnormal people. They know he or she is a little odd but they're treated, in a way, as part of the community. They do odd little jobs, some of the kids make fun of them and laugh at them. But people are rather kindly toward them, people aren't scared. This is not a large, impersonal urban society. So, in a way, the small community looks after them. In many of the villages I visited, I asked about people who were odd. When I first went to Japan, this was not at all an unusual pattern.

Another common pattern in Japan were these small hospitals which individual doctors have at their homes, ten-, fifteen-, twenty-bed hospitals which a doctor runs like a small enterprise. Quite a few of these doctors looked after mentally disturbed people and, except for Masazawa Hospital, the large mental hospital in Tokyo, there really were very few mental hospitals of any size then. Psychiatry at that time had also been largely German-influenced, so it was overwhelmingly physiological. And there was very little interest in psychology —in clinical psychology or in psychoanalysis.

Takeo Doi used to say whenever he ran into American psychiatrists they would ask: "Why are the Japanese so peculiar that they have no interest in psychoanalysis?" He used to reply that it was a fascinating question but a more interesting question was why one society, namely the

United States, was so peculiar as to have such a fascination with psychoanalysis.

Since that time, of course, there has been a growing interest here in psychological problems. The tiny cult of largely Western-educated people interested in psychoanalysis in 1958 has since grown to a fairly substantial size. There is today quite a growth in the mental health professions in Japan.

BK: What is the psychological orientation of the Japanese? Are they Freudian?

EV: Well, even in the United States, there's been a turn against Freud. He's not quite as popular as he was in his heyday, maybe ten to fifteen years ago. In Japan there's a very small group, really, that's very interested in the Freudian approach. But there's a lot more discussion of mental problems and difficulties in adjustment. Or, to view it in another way, in the history of the United States there was a period when social work was the responsibility of richer people, who were comfortable in the society and felt it was their responsibility to help out. It has only been in the twentieth century—the twenties, thirties and after World War II—that, in the United States, we really professionalized social work and developed all types of special training for it.

I believe Japan went through the same thing in the sixties and the seventies, in a very telescoped period. Yet well into the sixties and even the seventies, however, a great many older Japanese people still feel responsible for giving advice and helping on a kind of a personal, informal, nonprofessional way. This is still much more common in Japan now than it is in the United States.

BK: Which society then do you think creates more psychological pressures?

EV: That's a tough question because there is a distinction between incidence and prevalence. When something breaks out—that's incidence. And prevalence means how common it is. The real question is: when do these things break out? The fact is we don't have the kind of good studies which track every new case of incidence in mental health in all countries, and it's almost impossible to work methodologically because there are so many people who just don't want those things to come to public attention.

But, in general, in the United States, I think what you can say is the pressures are of a different kind than in Japan. In Japan, pressures are very much group pressures, for instance to succeed at the entrance examinations and make the grade; the pressures to succeed over certain hurdles, such as getting into the right company. They're fantastic. And when people don't succeed, the impact is very obvious.

In the United States, if anything, we are a less structured society. So we often don't have the group support and people kind of drift. There is the emptiness of not having things around us to support us. On the other hand, the group pressure of other young people on taking drugs or other kinds of things, these peer pressures are very strong in the US. Furthermore, there are the complicated heterosexual relationships, especially for young people. The fact that American society is so unstructured creates many of the problems; for example the opportunities of married people to have affairs or just friendships with people of the opposite sex often creates conflicts and cross-pressures that are really very difficult in the US, while these things are in a way under greater control here because there is more of a social structure in Japan.

BK: But aren't the life-long pressures much greater in Japan? The first hurdle is getting into the right school or latching on to the right job. But isn't it quite suffocating after that? The rituals involved with marriage; the limitations a wife faces in the marital relationship that no Western wife would put up with; the group pressures to conform, to hold back on one's real views and intentions, the fact that in a vertically-structured life-long employment system you are always working for the same people and must adjust to them even if you don't like them; you just can't escape. Plus the crowded living, the long commutes. This adds up to considerable pressure—almost a life of 'quiet desperation,' does it not? Doesn't it create neurosis?

EV: The prevalence or the incidence is very hard to compare, symptomatically. The things you described are certainly very real. I guess the situation in Japan, is maybe slightly better than you described. Because, number one, I think the hour and a half commute is largely a Tokyo phenomenon; to some extent also an Osaka one. But in the middle-sized and the smaller cities, it's not as strong and once you get outside those elite groups, I believe the pressures, particularly in the cities other than Tokyo and Osaka, are generally not quite as great on most people.

Also, while there may be a lot of tension and hostility and rivalry, there's also a lot of group support. I am constantly impressed at really how much camaraderie there is, and how much people actually let their hair down and talk in a friendly and supportive way. I'm inclined to universities. Compare it to Harvard. At Harvard people are very independent; they do their own thing. In a way its very close to the old frontier; a modern version of the frontier. Our corporations may give a little more mutual support than there is in a university. In Japan however, in the corporate life of the people I know, and among the groups of men I go out drinking with, I find a tremendous group support. You see familiarity, laughing and joking, and considerateness in a way that you don't find elsewhere.

BK: But people don't speak up very much in the formal or in the business situation. There's very little open argument or controversy. In the company, if you strongly oppose something, you may show your displeasure by putting your *hanko* upside-down, or by not answering the question, but nobody really says, "by God, this idea is crazy, and if we go through with this, we're gonna lose a million dollars," or, "you know, you must be out of your mind to suggest that we do this or that." People don't talk that way even if that's what they must be thinking.

EV: In most cases, though, there are acceptable ways of saying that at an earlier stage before it reaches that point.

Usually, in a Japanese company when some outrageous idea gets proposed it doesn't get to the final stage without a lot of tossing around. There are ways of asking questions; there are also ways of saying: you know, "there might be problems you run into," without actually saying "I oppose what you're doing." That can create doubts, or require further discussion, or require that ideas go through other rounds, or necessitate outside views.

I was quite impressed that in Japanese factories, for example, a higher-up person doesn't feel threatened by comments from a lower-status person because his job is not at stake. Everyone knows their position: therefore, the lower-status person can come up and speak quite frankly; the higher person doesn't fear just because the lower-status person is very bright that he's going to try to take over his job.

In the United States, however, because there is more mobility, if you argue, you might quit or get fired. There's also always the possibility in the US that a relationship will flip; in Japan relationships are longer-lasting. It's very rare that relationships develop in such a way that one divorces one's present spouse. But in the United States, again, we can never be sure. There are somehow more uncertainties about all those things because boundaries aren't as firm and tight. That creates tensions of its own.

BK: Are the Japanese and Americans different as people? Or is it just a difference in the cultural environment?

For instance you cannot really push a Japanese into a corner; Japanese society doesn't allow for that. If you do push a Japanese into a corner, he probably goes berserk. If you pushed someone out of a business or if you fired someone outright, that's almost suicide, isn't it?

EV: Yes.

BK: Well is that cultural, or are the Japanese a different breed?

Ezra Vogel

EV: You know, when I try to explain things to Americans who are visiting Japan for the first time, and who don't know much about the country and want to know how to behave, my first impulse is to say, "you know, the Japanese are really quite human." And my first prescription is, you know, by and large, "behave as you would, in a considerate way, toward anybody else." And, I think that goes very far. The Japanese, maybe through television and movies, are quite familiar with the West now. They are quite Westernized. So, there are a lot of similarities already.

But, there are still some cultural differences. Yet some things I thought were really cultural twenty, thirty, years ago, are no longer cultural now. When I first went to Japan, families I met would discuss *tatami*, how much they loved *tatami*, how it was the Japanese way of doing things; "we've always, had this, it's softer," etc, and the floral culture, the whole thing. Yet ten years later when I came back to the same house there was a carpet. When I remarked, "Well, why do you have a carpet?" the response was: "Well, it's more convenient."

People who were sitting on the floor before now sit on chairs. There have been similar changes in personality; people who did not express disagreement, say twenty-five years ago, now have learned how to express disagreement. Like kids in families, and the parents have learned how to respond to them without blowing up and have it all fall apart.

BK: Will Japan continue to change further and become more and more Westernized?

EV: Japan is in a real dilemma as I see it now. It has made an extraordinary adjustment to the West but it has still a kind of buffer zone between the West and itself. Foreigners are kept in a certain sense not completely ghettoized, but still, confined to certain places. Foreigners don't run around, they aren't all over Japanese companies, they don't come into the center of Japanese companies and the center of Japanese life. And many of the Japanese who go abroad to learn about the West in a way don't come back to the center of Japanese companies, either. They become kind of specialists, who know English, know about the West but are not quite incorporated into Japanese life.

And then there's this cosmopolitan group of Japanese friends whom you know and I know, who have learned how to interact with the West, who can interpret and tell other Japanese about the West, and yet contribute to keep large parts of this society closed where outsiders don't penetrate, such as their social clubs, for example.

I can remember going to some Japanese business organizations and being told: "Gosh, I'm sorry, I didn't think they'd invite you to our group. I mean we never have foreigners, and there isn't any, you know, anything special about it, we just don't do it!" Sometimes I've been invited to those groups which until now never had foreigners. But, even if you had one or two foreigners, it doesn't really change the nature of it; we don't shake the place.

So what Japan confronts now is a new stage of contact with the outside where that buffer zone is no longer going to work so well. The level of contact with the outside is going to increase considerably from now on. And the number of foreigners who can operate in Japan, either with or without the language, is increasing. A number of foreign organizations are also going to be operating in Japan, hiring Japanese people away from Japanese firms, competing for talent, being involved in takeovers. A number of Japanese are going to be stationed overseas for a substantial length of time and the close interaction with foreigners is going to grow. This buffer zone is no longer going to be able to contain the level of contact with the outside. And, how they're going to deal with that is going to be one of the really big problems in the next decade or two. One could imagine that foreigners may come in to Japan to such an extent that many of these organizations will no longer be able to maintain their closedness. Like the press clubs, for example, which thus far have figured out clever devices for keeping foreigners out—such as having the foreigners at their own

114

press club, so they can still maintain their own press club in their quiet way.

BK: I can probably contribute a few more examples to your list. A newly-founded cable-TV company applied to the Postal Ministry for a license and had an American on its board. The ministry quietly let it be known the company would never get its license if they didn't get rid of the foreigner so he was asked to become an advisor.

EV: That's still very prominent, all over the place. And, at a time when Japan runs such a large trade imbalance. I think Japan is going to be in more trouble internationally than they realize. They still seem to feel if you just send people abroad and explain how foreigners don't understand this and get rid of the misunderstandings, well then everything will be all right. But it is significantly different when they run such a big trade imbalance. I think the Reagan administration gave them a little breathing spell for political reasons. But it's not going to last in the United States and it's not going to last in Europe. From now on the Japanese are going to be under a lot of pressure.

BK: I was surprised the Reagan administration, of all administrations, took that stance. The Houdaille case was a good example. Reagan caved in so easily.

EV: Yes.

BK: Had the administration gone through with it, as unfair as it might have seemed, it wouldn't actually have hurt that many people and it would have sent some message to Japan that you just can't play it both ways.

EV: But obviously, you know, Reagan wanted to show, before the election, that he was a big statesman, and that Nakasone had been very helpful to him at the summit meeting by making a big anti-Soviet statement. That's why he caved in. And Reagan, you know, tries to stay above politics, but the political pressures in the United States, particularly with the downturn in the economy, sometime in the next year or two, will create a very different environment. And these things about Japan will come under much greater scrutiny. And the Japanese will look very bad if they send people abroad to explain as if everything was all right when all those things still continue to go on.

BK: It's *deja vu*, isn't it?

EV: It really is. And I believe it will escalate. It's the same kind of thing they were doing in 1941, when they sent people over to explain things, and were actually planning Pearl Harbor. They haven't cleaned up their act at home, yet they're sending people abroad to explain. Well, it's pretty bad.

BK: I just wonder what the next three or four years will be like. Have we nearly reached the peak of Mt. Fuji and are we going to de-escalate the problems soon?

EV: It's so hard, it's so hard. All of us are constantly looking for solutions and none of us has any secret answer. None of us are fortune-tellers. I guess, however, I've been surprised at a couple of things. One is when I felt things were getting so bad I thought that they would continue to get worse, and then the Reagana administration pulled back. This suggests there are a lot of very powerful forces on both sides that want to keep the thing under control. Another, a whole new kind of thing that is happening now: there are so many agreements between so many different American companies and so many different Japanese companies that everybody has to pull their punches. In a way, they're in bed with each other, whether they like it or not. General Motors isn't going to come out strongly in favor of protection against Japanese cars because they are now involved in importing a great many cars from Japan. Many other American companies which used to manufacture predominantly in the United States are now earning part of their money by selling goods that come from Japan. When you have that complex pattern of cooperation, even while they compete, it makes it much more difficult to maintain a state of protectionism.

At the same time, the fact that they're holding full cabinet meetings to discuss Japanese import/export problems, the trade balance, suggests the seriousness with which the administration is looking at the issue. Although we know the balances are going to be very one-sided, when they're announced it still will carry considerable weight. And then, a year or two later when our economy will be in even more trouble, as I think it will be, they're going to be a lot more serious about US-Japanese problems. We're borrowing too much money and living off the borrowed money; it just can't keep up.

BK: Have you ever envisioned Japan taking a ninety degree turn under certain situations? I'm changing the subject slightly, but are they capable of suddenly moving in a totally different direction as a result of a security or an economic crisis?

EV: What kind of ninety degree turn? What would be an example?

BK: Well, there certainly was a ninety degree turn, say, toward militarism before World War II and then suddenly a total abandonment of militarism and a concentration on economic pursuits.

EV: I guess what I see as much more likely is yielding at the last minute before something explodes. I mean, for example, where you would think they would never open up X, Y and Z, to foreigners, they might, under considerable foreign pressure, yield. You may believe the Japanese aren't going to do X-Y-Z, but they may begin doing it. So I think rather that they will yield to a lot of pressure because it's hard to see what kind of ninety degree turn they could take now. I suppose one of the big questions is; could they go independent? Could they be more independent in military development? Could that really escalate? I believe they will have an increased military but I just don't see independence. They still need to rely on the United States for nuclear cover and they're also so dependent on the United States for exports, and for goodwill. Also, so many of their energy supplies come, if not from the United States, then through a kind of multinational arrangement which involves the

United States. There are so many ways in which they are now so dependent on the rest of the world and the world is now too crowded that I just don't think there is any room to make a sharp ninety degree turn.

BK: But, if they were threatened—as they were in 1973—with an oil crisis, and I recall quite vividly the time when Kissinger was here and Nakasone and all these top figures were all there in the American Embassy for some reception, eagerly asking Kissinger to give them some guarantees. Right at the reception they went out into the Embassy courtyard, begging for a guarantee that the US would continue to supply Japan with oil if their lines were cut. And Kissinger wouldn't guarantee anything that evening. I mean that kind of critical situation. And Nakasone, who was MITI minister, was proposing internally that Japan consider cutting its ties with Israel. Don't you see the possibility of the Japanese moving in whatever direction permits them to get what they need?

EV: They're so dependent on the United States, I can't see them going independent from the United States because they really need us.

BK: What if we abandoned them? Or if they perceived that we were abandoning them?

EV: I guess it's hard for me to imagine America abandoning Japan. We're now, also our companies are now, so dependent on so much technology and there is so much intermeshing. Many major corporations are involved in joint production—airplanes produced in the United States contain so many parts that are now made in Japan that we don't really have the capacity to produce them. I just don't see that that's possible, in the same way that it would have been, say, twenty or thirty years ago.

BK: I understand; however, Japan nearly cut ties with Israel during the oil crisis of 1973 but was restrained by such cool heads as Eimei Yamashita, then the MITI vice minister.

EV: I don't think it was just Yamashita Eimei; I think they also realized a lot of the majors are connected with the

United States. They couldn't get all the oil they wanted just from the Arab countries; they depended also on the United States. And before they suddenly cut relations with Israel, they would have to consider what that is going to do to the oil supply from the United States. They just don't have that leverage. Even though some people would have liked to have done it, the fact is they couldn't. Just too much of that is controlled by the United States. Or, put it another way: the world has internationalized so much in the last twelve years in foreign trade, mutual involvement, the complex network, that you can't disengage in the same way you could in the '30s, and even the '50s. It's almost like saying you could disengage Massachusetts from New Hampshire. There's just too great a constant flow of people and traffic back and forth.

BK: You can't move the geography.

EV: Yes, and besides there's television, the press: It's just a tremendously interdependent world. Even the hot-heads under pressure who might be tempted to break some of the relationships will find that they can't really go nearly as far as they would like to. In balance that's a very good thing for the world. Since we're so intermeshed now nobody can pull out. But, on the other hand, the pressure will certainly be on Japan much more strongly henceforth to play the game in the same way as the rest of the world does.

BK: Let's go back and talk about *Japan as Number One*. I recall you asked me to read the manuscript in draft form in 1978.

EV: I remember you did, yes. You were very helpful, too.

BK: Well, it was a great success. How has it been? What are some of your perceptions about its success and in what sense do you think you were either understood or misunderstood by your readers or critics? Was it perceived as what you had intended it to be, or did it become something more than that?

EV: In the United States, it was very much as it was

intended. It meant to say: "Look, boys, here's a very powerful country, and there's a lot to learn from them." Although some of the reactions at first among some intellectuals and academics were very restrained, I mean they said that it didn't talk enough about cultural differences and if our culture was so different, we couldn't learn from it, it did help to set in motion an effort to learn from the Japanese, which made common sense. Conservative businessmen, who don't particularly like Japan, agreed there was something to be learned from them: we can't copy them but there are things to be learned in the manufacturing systems such as the "just in time" process or the effort to attain better cooperation between government and business. A lot of such things were set in motion so that the book attained its objective.

In Japan, however, it was't quite as I intended because it wasn't written primarily for a Japanese audience. However it became a symbol in Japan, for something. A great many people knew the title but didn't know the book. In the preface of the book, for example, in the Japanese preface, I wrote that one must beware of the dangers of excessive pride, which is what ruined the United States. I also said the Japanese had many problems, and must be very cautious about them. But by and large, that didn't turn out to be the Japanese image of the book. The large public image was that here is a Harvard professor, who awards the prize, like somebody giving a rating, sitting out there judging, and here Japan gets the top prize. And so we're wonderful, we're all right, and other countries are all wrong. I think it was used in that way to some extent in Japan, and that was of course not as I intended it.

BK: Have you changed your thesis or theory in any way about Japan?

EV: I've changed not so much my interpretation of Japan, as I have as to what America ought to do. There are some things I said in the last chapter that America ought to do which I no longer advocate. One of the main things I advocated is that we ought to have a strong, elite bureaucracy to deal with industrial structure problems. I found, however, as I lectured across the country, that when I talked about America having a bureaucratic elite it was not popular, to say the least. And even when I modified that to specialists working on industrial strategy to guide our government's policy, people were very suspicious. The more I talked to people who really knew about our governmental processes, the more I was convinced we can't have anything like a MITI.

BK: They don't want any of those Harvard guys up there in Washington?

EV: That's right. And, you know, *The Wall Street Journal* had an article reviewing Bob Reich's book, *The Next American Frontier*, which I think put it very well: we finally deregulated and got those God-damned Harvard lawyers out of here! And now these guys are trying to find another way to get back in here, under the guise of "industrial policy." In the US?

So, there is the revulsion against an elite bureaucracy that is just so strong, business simply would not accept it. Secondly, we don't have a tradition of restraint; it would be so easy for political groups to gain control and steer the thing in the wrong direction. What I've tried to do in my new book, *Comeback*, is to spell-out a proposal for an American response to the Japanese economic challenge. Whereas *Japan is Number One* was sort of a broad sweep at government, information-gathering, education, crime control, etc, this is more exclusively on the economy, and particularly business and government, and what they ought to be doing about it.

In trying to think through the issue, I found that we can do a lot of things short of having a bureaucracy. For example, the American government could bring together councils of business leaders to think about certain issues, and to try to gather business opinion. We could develop a lot more competitive analysis in Washington and give that much greater prominence in our policy. In fact, there are a whole series of things that we can do: encourage not only new kinds of scientific research but also application, give tax credits for rapid application of new technology, etc. These could make a difference. So, I guess that's more or less where I come out, and that's significant. It's a few degrees difference from where I was six or seven years ago. I got letters from many people after *Japan is Number One* but even though there were many little differences of opinion, I didn't hear anything that really made me want to change what I said. If anything I think time has sort of supported the kind of things I was arguing. In fact, many things I wrote five years ago seemed somewhat crazy and way-out then but have now become the accepted wisdom.

For example what I said about how well the Japanese were doing in all kinds of areas are now topped out in speeches even by American politicians as being just the way it is. So, while there's not much I would want to change, I would want to add a lot more qualifications which call more attention to the Japanese weaknesses. I mentioned those and I believe I covered myself in writing about them in the book, but I would probably want—if I were writing that same book over—to have expanded that section, because many people went through the book without noticing that aspect.

BK: What are some of those weaknesses?

EV: One is the lack of being international; the Japanese are probably too inward-looking. Another thing, the downside of the big organizations, is the tremendous pressure against nonconformity; it's very difficult for people who don't fit in. They don't have enough space for deviance. Things are often not sufficiently flexible. They are too tough on people who have little differences of opinion or ideas. They are not tolerant enough. They're over-structured.

BK: How many copies did the book sell, both here and in Japan?

EV: The Japanese language edition sold 600,000 copies. In the United States, the hardback passed 30,000. The paperback in the United States sold around 100,000. In

Japan, there was also an English edition brought out by Tuttle and that may have sold up to 100,000 so far. And then there were pirated editions printed in Indonesia, Korea, Taiwan and Mainland China.

BK: Did you claim?

EV: No, because they aren't participants in international copyright law, so it's not illegal. But there were five different publishers in Taiwan that did it. And there was at least one in Mainland China which published it. There were also Portuguese, Spanish, and French editions. In Taiwan and Singapore, the cabinets were required to read it. Lee Kwan-Yew ordered his cabinet to read it, and so did Chiang Ching-kuo, I heard, on Taiwan. So it got a lot of publicity in those places.

BK: That reminds me: I once bought a copy of one of Reischauer's books in Taiwan, and when he left Japan at a farewell lunch for him at the Foreign Correspondents Club in Tokyo, I asked him to autograph that copy. But he wrote: to Bernard Krishauer, or something like that, from Edwin F. Reichour —H-O-U-R. He explained: pirated books didn't deserve a genuine autograph. Anyway, that's a real collector's item for me. But how has fame and wealth changed your life?

EV: I haven't become as rich as some people think. The Harvard Press got half of the royalties from Japan. I hadn't even thought about it in those days. But, indirectly when I lecture, I can make money off the book, and now, my next book will get more attention and more of an advance because of the last one. It's taken financial worry out of my mind.

BK: I heard the first royalty helped you remodel your Cambridge house.

EV: Oh yes! The royalties paid for re-making this house. This house would be in very bad shape today if it hadn't been for that book. It sort of takes the edge off things. The fact that I can relax and not worry about financial things, that's nice. Fame gets you things. Maybe it shouldn't be that way but I find people take me more seriously. When I go places, and when I'm interviewed, I don't have to explain who I am.

BK: But Harvard always had a big cachet.

EV: Harvard always meant a lot, that's true, especially in East Asia.

BK: And in the States?

EV: In the States, I don't think it means nearly as much as it did. Fame, I think everywhere, in terms of what you're trying to do, opens more doors and gets people to listen to you more than otherwise. Now that I've had both experiences I could argue on either side. I used to feel there were many big Harvard names working very hard who did not get any attention. I felt that was very unfair. I suppose those people now would say the same thing about me. But, on the whole, it hasn't created problems with colleagues. Maybe because it came to me late enough in life that it sort of cuts younger people apart. And, as far as I can tell, it also hasn't affected old relationships at all. One of the problems, however, is that it forces a lot of new choices; you have a lot of opportunities to take part in conferences which are hard to refuse.

BK: How has it conflicted with your teaching?

EV: Well, that is a problem. In the past, I never went to Asia during the academic year, from September to June. But, last year, the opportunity to be a speaker at the Fifth Generation Computer Conference in Tokyo and to follow that forefront technology which I'm very interested in was hard to refuse, so I did that. Governor Dukakis took a trip to Japan and China this year and asked me to go with him. Again, this keeps a lot of doors open and is interesting. It's the kind of opportunity I didn't have before.

There's no question about it, it does take time away from the students. I can't be quite as leisurely with them as I was and I'm a little more harassed. I have to take off, other people have to fill in for me. So far, there are enough people around here of the younger age groups. But one of the problems with Harvard is that we don't have enough people working on contemporary Asia. So, I'm overstretched. If we had more people working on contemporary Asia here it wouldn't be as much of a problem because it could be more easily shared. Yet I'm glad I have this opportunity. I didn't seek it when I wrote the book, I hadn't thought through all these things; I just had a message that I wanted to get across.

The invitations do create conflicts of time and it's easy to get on a treadmill so one has to learn how to say no. I used to accept most reasonable speaking engagements but I've learned how to say no to a lot of things. For example, the local Japanese consul general is forever frustrated with me because there are so many Japanese visitors coming through here and he would like me to greet all of them. But there's no way I can do my job, see students in the university and greet all the visitors. There isn't any resident "American friend of Japan" in the Boston area and for all these big occasions they always expect me to turn out, and I just can't do it.

BK: To move to another theme: on a personal basis, have you ever been disappointed by a Japanese?

EV: Well, there were people I knew, for example, at Harvard, who were one thing when they were at Harvard and totally changed to another thing when they returned to their bureaucratic posts in Japan. Some of them became very narrow defendants of their bureaucratic positions. Or, another example: a Japanese friend who wanted to cooperate in all kinds of things, and proposed "let's do this," and "let's do that," suddenly disappeared when I started to want to implement them. Those experiences were very disappointing.

BK: Were these people devious or arrogant, or what?

EV: As an American I thought we had really developed a relationship and I expected them to respond in a certain way, but then I learned: their public responsibility in their organization or government or whatever came first and defined how they thought they had to behave, and they behaved that way; in a way that seemed to me to be out of keeping with the way friends behave toward each other. The thing is that role pressures in work are very strong, and that stands in the way of personal relationships.

BK: The idea then that in Japan personal relations are everything and a person will die for his classmate, etc, is a myth. Can you name other myths?

EV: The myth of the mother school. Take the strong bond among Tokyo University graduates, the "Tokyo clique;" yet, ask these same people, what they're doing for Tokyo University: they don't give a damn about what happens to Todai. The loyalty to the old school is surprisingly weak. I would have also thought that many people would spend a lot of time seeing each other after retiring from a company. Yet, they don't see each other at all. I was really quite surprised, after everything that's said about Japanese loyalty, and how their whole life centers around it, how completely they cut off old relationships.

BK: Is self-interest then really the basis of loyalty? And when self-interest isn't served, loyalty dissipates?

EV: Yes, self-interest is very powerful in Japan. Or, self-interest related to the organization. And, while they may try to hide it, if you look at what the Japanese actually do, you can see, it's very powerful.

On the other hand, there are a lot of other relationships where I have found people to be extremely loyal and helpful, way beyond what you would expect. This is ten, twenty, twenty-five years later, where you couldn't possibly have any organizational motive, only old feelings of friendship.

The persons I've had the most difficulties and disappointments with are the operators, people who are success-bound, going and rising ahead, who feel they've got to push ahead in their organization to achieve certain positions.

BK: Is Japan beginning to lose something as it's becoming ever more successful and efficient?

Is it no longer as attractive as in 1958 or 1959 when you first discovered it?

Ezra Vogel

EV: Actually, I guess I've been rather surprised how much of that they still have. I mean, how strong some friendships or relationships still are; how much they care about people. For example, Talcott Parsons, a Harvard sociology professor, wasn't considered so important anymore at Harvard after retirement. Yet, when he came to Japan, even though he didn't teach there anymore, they still treated him very graciously: a senior man, with honor. Or Kevin White, who was our mayor here until recently, he said he just got back from Japan and they were so kind to him; they acted as if he were still mayor. You know what I mean? They obviously knew he had no position or power. They didn't expect anything from him but they regarded him as an older, senior person; someone they feel they should treat with a certain graciousness and kindness. I've been impressed at how much there still is of that.

BK: But sometimes they also falsely consider a person out of power as still having power.

EV: That's true, that's true. But still there's also a kindness toward older people. You don't just dump 'em and throw 'em on the rubbish heap. That's true in Japan, and it's also true toward foreigners.

BK: Look at Mansfield.

EV: Yes. They love him. He'd never get that kind of treatment in any other country.

BK: Who, finally, would you say you admire most among the Japanese—present or past?

EV: Let's start with the present. The person I admire most is Toshio Doko. I think he is a man of just absolute integrity. He possesses a real kind of religious commitment and through a simple, plain life. And for a person who has been through so much power, to behave with such sincerity, and to work with such dedication, to try to keep down, you know, Japanese spending—I mean, just compare him with somebody like Stockman! He just has so much more depth and dedication. He has just about everything. He has an engineering background and he had been on top of the business community, he gives his money to charity and he lives very simply; I just find him an extraordinarily dedicated and wonderful person.

I also found (former Prime Minister) Masayoshi Ohira a wonderful man as a Japanese politician. I know Reischauer also felt that Ohira was a very special person, absolutely sincere, maybe not always the most articulate, but very thoughtful and loyal. Someone who did not speak with a forked tongue. He was always absolutely straight.

Let's see, who are some of the other Japanese I admire? Among the young intellectuals, Sato Seizabuno is an extraordinary person. I admire him so much not only because he is so bright, and so quick and so effective and so close to power, but because he is a genuine internationalist. He has been extremely gracious and helpful to a large number of foreign students at all levels. He really is very impressive. Takeshi Ishida is another one. Those two academics, I think, have probably been more helpful to more foreign scholars than anybody I know here. There are many others like that but those two, really, particularly, are very genuine internationalists and very dedicated and committed. And at the other end of the pole, there are also people who I don't admire.

BK: Who?

EV: Some of the sleazy people, like Sasagawa Ryoichi and Kodama Toshio, people like that. It's hard to have as much respect for them.

BK: What about Tanaka Kakuei?

EV: I find Tanaka a more complex figure. I guess I would be more forgiving of Tanaka than many Americans because, from what I know, he's extremely able and loyal to people he knows. He's extraordinarily dedicated to people in his district. He's not a nasty person. He's not a villainous kind of person who destroys others for the sake of his own career, as far as I am aware. He hasn't abided by things we consider to be the canons of honesty, or of public integrity. But, from his view, he was looking after the interests of his people. He's very loyal to the people under him, and charming. He somewhat reminds me of the old-style Irish politician in Boston.

BK: Then a real final question—which society is better, Japanese or American society?

EV: Japanese society is more effective right now. But, I would rather live in America, and maybe it's because I'm American; I'm more comfortable with American society. There is a certain generosity from Americans toward the rest of the world, and a certain openness by American society toward the world, a concern about the world, which I don't find in Japan. On the other hand, the effectiveness in giving very good training to children, of keeping the place safe and clean and running on time, and providing a kind of style of life, that's also important for people. People in Japanese organizations get enormous support from their organizations. There's concern. People help each other. I wish we had more of that in the United States. So, I guess—like all of us who have lived in both societies—we see good and bad points in each one, and that's probably why I chose to live in America, but I still admire an awful lot about Japan. I wish we could keep some of our best qualities and at the same time I wish we could learn how to run things a little better, to be more like them.

"The Japanese made an important decision at the end of the war to become democratic capitalists."

Bernard Krisher: How did you become connected to Japan?

Robert Christopher: It started purely by accident. My father urged me to take a Japanese course at college because this was 1941. He said I think we're going to have a war with Japan and it would be useful to know Japanese in the army. So I did. Shortly after the war broke out the Army did in fact come to collect me and sent me to Japanese language school. At the end of the war I came here immediately after the surrender and was just fascinated by the place and I've remained so ever since.

BK: What do you recall about your first exposure to Japan?

RC: Well, we landed at Atsugi; we flew up from Okinawa and my first impression was one of astonishment, at how primitive everything was. The Japanese army, the Japanese government, had lined up a whole bunch of trucks to transport us to Yokohama, the first headquarters. The trucks looked like something that might have been built in the States in the twenties, they were very very old-fashioned and rugged. Then the houses. It's one thing to read about houses with glazed paper windows, made of wood and so forth, and it's something else to actually see them. And the people working in the fields, peasants. You know, I'd never seen a peasant in my life.

And suddenly I realized although we had been fighting a very formidable military machine indeed, when you got to the homeland of this military machine, it turned out to be remarkably rural and unadvanced in a technical sense.

BK: Had you come equipped with some insights about Japan, *The Chrysanthemum and the Sword* ?

RC: No, *The Chrysanthemum and the Sword* hadn't been published yet; it wasn't published until late '45 or early '46. We didn't have a lot of insights, just what we had learned through talking to Japanese prisoners, which I had done. And some insights gained from my commanding officer, Ed Reischauer, who had given us the cultural-

Robert Christopher

historical background. Yet nothing really prepared me for the fact that the technical and industrial level of the country was as low and narrow as it was.

I still remember driving along through the rice fields and as we approached the city we began to see the results of the bombing. It was the most depressing sight you could imagine. I never had any idea that that kind of destruction could be inflicted on a community.

BK: What kept you interested in Japan all these years?

RC: Several things. I just have a taste for the exotic if you will, always have had, from the time I was a child. Any community, any society other than my own interested me. But with Japan the differences are so significant that they help to cast a new perspective on your own society.

Also the constant change in the society fascinated me; although I've never lived here for any long period—the longest stretch I was ever here was for a year—I come back a lot and the constant change in the society is fascinating. And, I just like the Japanese. I like Japan. I find them interesting, engaging people. They're sympathetic, as far as I'm concerned.

BK: What moved Japan so rapidly from what you saw in 1945 to what Japan has become today? It's a remarkable achievement but what are the ingredients?

RC: To come down to cliches, I'm afraid, one thing is the group orientation of the Japanese and the way in which that effects them. They are reluctant to let the team down, so they work enormously hard and skillfully, not simply out of personal ambition, but in order not to let the team down, if you will, not to become cast out by the team. Another thing is they are working essentially for shared goals a lot of the time, rather than for purely individual ones. Fewer policies are made to suit somebody's personal ambitions than is true in most societies.

In a funny way the Japanese made an essential decision at the end of the war to become democratic capitalists. I just happen to believe that capitalism and a democratic society is one of the most effective forms of organization known to man if it's managed intelligently and with some sense of responsibility.

The Japanese have given free play to the dynamic forces in capitalism, but always with a sense of overall social responsibility. As a result, they've been able to take techniques of various kinds, not just industrial, which we taught them, and apply them more effectively than we ourselves apply them.

BK: The Japanese seem to be unique in the world. There are no other people, there is no other society, though Korea as a Confucian society resembles them, that appear to have achieved this. Are they a different species, that God put on this earth? Or, are there more mundane reasons for the particular way they behave?

RC: A lot of people use the point you just mentioned, the key one, the Confucian influence on Japanese thinking and society, and I think it is very important. It's important in Korea and in Taiwan and in Chinese Singapore as well; yet, although those societies are doing or have done well economically, none of them is a democratic society. Japan in my view really is.

And as to just why that's so I can only conjecture. I believe it goes back to this business of having always been a place where decisions were made by the group, or at least a strong man who was always constrained by group opinion. It's not very satisfactory but it's the only explanation I can come up with.

BK: Does geography or the fact that they are an island country lacking in resources play a factor?

RC: To a large extent. There were a combination of factors which made this a very unpromising and difficult place for people to live.

Natural disasters were frequent, there weren't very many natural resources, and, for reasons that I don't know or understand, the country has been heavily populated for centuries, so that in a sense you had to have some kind of cooperative action or else you were going to have bloody chaos. They are very pragmatic, common-sense people in my view.

BK: What would you say are some of the qualities the Japanese society possesses which the rest of the world might well emulate if it could?

RC: The way in which the Japanese combine individual freedom with social responsibility is one. Another is the curious kind of political stability they have had since World War II, allowing for interplay between rival groups but containing the rivalry within very fixed limits. Japan is also really very much an equal opportunity society to a much greater extent really than European societies or even the American society.

BK: Some examples?

RC: Well, the fact that you don't really inherit status or power in this country in a meaningful way. Nothing like the way it happens in the United States or much less in Europe. Sure, a poor kid has a chance in the United States, but I think he has a better chance in Japan. He has a better chance of making it all the way because there is more of a meritocracy.

BK: How much of what is worth emulating in Japanese society is really capable of being absorbed by other societies?

RC: There are obviously very real limits on what we can absorb. There is no way, for example, that you'll get individualistic Americans to behave like group-oriented Japanese. But there are things we can do in the United States which would in a way emulate the Japanese and which are not incompatible with individualism.

For example, our industrial managerial class has become much too arrogant. It's overpaid; it regards itself as sort of an elite and thus pays very little attention to workers and to motivating workers. If you could reduce the kind of class distinction between executives and blue collar people in the States it would help a lot. Another thing we could do is pay more attention to making ordinary working class people feel their contribution is meaningful, that they are not just interchangeable parts.

BK: What are the psychic sacrifices which the Japanese have to make that Westerners might not be willing to make to have the kind of society that the Japanese have?

RC: Well, Westerners might be reluctant to give up the concept, as the song goes, "I did it my way..." and I don't think Americans, at least, would be content with being just a cog in a machine.

BK: Also, the sense of restraint, the misdirected communications, the *honne* and *tatemae* and all of this, this *kabuki*, but could a Westerner stand that for more than an hour without blurting out what he really thinks?

RC: Not the way we're brought up now and I think probably you couldn't really impose it on Westerners. I think that to try to create a similar society, with as many constraints as this one has socially, in the Western world would be extremely difficult and probably impossible. But that isn't to say that we couldn't cooperate with each other a bit more than we do. And that we couldn't attach somewhat greater importance to achieving collective goals than we now do.

BK: What mental strain does this kind of behavior have on the Japanese?

RC: A lot I think. One trivial example in a way, but maybe it isn't: the fact that you see so much public drunkenness on the part of substantial people in this country. It seems to me this is an evidence of a psychic strain. That's letting off steam that accumulates because of all the constraints.

Also, the occasional outbursts of irrational violence; we have those in the States too and everywhere in the world, but it seems to me that they occur here in kind of magnified form and particularly among young people. It's a manifestation of the terrible burden imposed by constraints. Like the kids who threw a firebomb in the LDP headquarters recently, or the kids who keep trying to blow up Narita, and these weird kind of awful obscure murders that occur among university students, for crazy ideological reasons.

BK: What are the qualities in Western society the Japanese might like to examine or adapt? Or would it be detrimental to their progress?

RC: Younger Japanese, it seems to me, are learning to be less reluctant to say 'no' than their parents were. If they think something is not workable they will say "no, I won't do that," rather than go into some song and dance and say "no, I'll take that into consideration."

I also know some Japanese in their twenties and thirties, particularly those who have worked abroad, who are showing a greater willingness to accept the fact that confrontation is sometimes a useful thing. I happen not to like confrontation myself and I find it very sympathetic that the Japanese dislike it so much, but it isn't a really workable way to behave in the world at large and I think the younger ones are beginning to realize it.

BK: Since your book has appeared, you've become an expert on Japan in America and an expert about America in Japan, and you've been talking to groups on both sides of the ocean.

What questions are most frequently asked in both societies about the other one and how do you respond to them?

RC: The question that Americans most often ask about Japanese right now is: "How do they do it?" It's this sense of bewilderment and wonderment in the States about Japan, that there must be some secret that they don't know, something about the Japanese they don't understand.

BK: And what do Japanese ask about Americans?

RC: It's funny, from Americans you tend to get broad philosophic questions about Japan, but from Japanese you tend to get very specific questions about the United States, like who's going to win the election, is protectionism going to continue to increase in the United States, what's Mr. Reagan going to do about this issue or that issue.

BK: So they already have the answers to the philosophical questions?

RC: Yes, for better or worse, rightly or wrongly, they know what the philosophical differences are; what they're interested in is the nitty gritty, as opposed to the Americans, who will either ask a kind of hostile question like why do the Japanese screw us, why do they dump these goods on us all the time, or they will ask, as I say, broad philosophical questions reflecting the fact that they really don't know much about this society.

BK: How do you gauge the press coverage of both societies, what you read in America about Japan and vice versa?

RC: In the United States, although it's improved somewhat, Japan is terribly undercovered; much of the coverage that does appear is inadequate or misleading, although it has improved some. But there just isn't enough of it and if you try to follow what's happening in Japan by reading only American publications it's like looking at the place through the wrong end of a telescope; you really have to know a lot about Japan to be able to interpret these fragments that appear. If anything, I would say the opposite is true in Japan where the United States is overcovered. They tend, because they cover the place like a blanket, to read too much significance into things that really don't have that much significance.

BK: What about journalism itself in Japan and in the US: which country is superior?

RC: I believe Japanese journalism is superior in one respect: they have enormous editorial resources. In the States a newspaper, or a magazine like Newsweek, is going through this right now; you get these enormous holddowns where you've got to do everything on the cheap. That doesn't happen with the Japanese.

In one area they really are markedly superior; that is in the coverage of their own government. There is no paper in the United States, no group of papers that cover the internal workings of the United States government as effectively as the Japanese newspapers do. If you're a Japanese citizen and you read the press faithfully you've got a very good idea of what's going on in the bureaucracy. You're not just suddenly presented with, "hey, there's a massive immigration bill that the Congress is going to decide on." From the moment that the subject begins to be a matter of concern to the bureaucracy, or whoever, it begins to be covered. Thus, the Japanese are much better informed about the operations of their own government. In general, the Japanese press, in terms of volume, does a lot more on the rest of the world than the United States does. I don't think it's always as good as it should be, or as balanced, but they do a lot more. The American press, however, is superior to the Japanese press in investigative reporting; the Japanese press it seems to me is very slow to blow the whistle on wrongdoing.

BK: The Japanese seem very concerned about communications and the communication gap. Do you see any improvement in person to person, business to business and government to government communications between Japan and other societies?

RC: I do see an improvement and I think at least to me its been most notable in the last few years, just on the level of the people who represent Japan in the United States, whether it's as ambassador or consul or the media representatives or whatever. They are a lot more sophisticated now than they were before and they deal with Americans a lot more easily. There are Japanese businessmen who operate in the American context much more effectively than any American businessman does in the Japanese context.

However, there still are certain problems. Maybe the Japanese are still relying too heavily on non-Japanese spokesmen in the States—and every now and then that gets some very unfavorable press, somebody will come around and say my God they are spending X hundred million dollars a year on propaganda in the United States. And not all of the people that they have doing it are all that good; some of them are hangovers from former administrations without any clout.

BK: If you were to advise Japanese business and government on the kind of people that they should engage to represent them in the US whom would you suggest?

RC: I don't much like to name names but I think to hire a deputy assistant secretary of balony from the previous administration is of very questionable value, particularly when it was of the other party. It creates a bad impression, it looks like they are trying to subvert the system somehow. I think they should rely on themselves more; they've got more and more people who can do it.

BK: Turning to your book. The Japanese Mind, for a moment—have you had any second thoughts about anything you've written.

RC: Sure. Obviously there are always a lot of things that one would modify, particularly when you're dealing with a country that changes as rapidly as this one does. The biggest thing that I regret about the book is that I didn't have one chunk of it that just talked about what appeared to be the directions of change. Because a lot of the things that I said, though true, are probably not going to be true ten, fifteen years from now.

BK: What changes do you foresee?

RC: In the broadest sense, the Japanese society will come to reflect much of the same values that let's say American society now has. I don't buy the argument that you hear in this country that ten years from now they all are going to be taking drugs and will be suffering from the British disease, economically. But I do think that changes in economic and industrial patterns tend to produce certain changes in social behavior, and it's happening here. The role of women, for example, is changing. I don't think you agree, but I just don't think that twenty years from now there is going to be nearly anything like as much difference as there is now between the role of women in this country and the role of women in the United States.

BK: What will this do to the society though?

RC: I don't know. It could be that it will change it very very dramatically, because obviously it affects child rearing. You could argue that because Mama isn't going to be home anymore that the whole society will change drastically. To some extent, there will be change for that reason. On the other hand, the whole thrust of the way Japanese children are brought up was always to socialize them, to make them good little members of the group. And maybe you can do that almost as effectively in a day care center as you can at Mama's knee. So, maybe the change won't be in the way children are brought up and won't be quite as dramatic as you might think.

In the States, it's been very dramatic. Because when they were brought up at home they were brought up with an individualistic thrust; when they go to day care centers they are brought up with a kind of group thrust. It's an interesting point not thought of: maybe we're going to come to resemble each other more, we're going to be a little less individualistic and they are going to be a little less group-oriented. I think there's going to be a greater resemblance between the two societies. The whole business of the role of women is central. I believe the Japanese family twenty years from now is going to be very close in its emotional and practical structure to the American family.

BK: What other changes do you foresee? What about Japan's role in the world?

RC: If the Japanese become, as I think they will, more adroit at dealing with the outside world, then I think they are going to obviously exercise greater political as well as economic clout. At some point, and I don't know when, the hesitancy they've had about using their power is going to begin to erode and they are going to start using it.

BK: Are you afraid of that?

RC: No not really afraid of it. I would be afraid of it if I thought they were going to exercise it in the same way they tried to exercise it in the '30s and '40s, but I don't think they will. They've become a lot more sophisticated; they are probably going to try to exercise their power the way that any other mature society exercises power.

BK: You may recall I had a memorable interview with Chie Nakane. Her response to a similar question was that the Japanese should not be given too much power or too much responsibility because they are a driven people. When they have a goal, they will set upon that goal with blinders on. Fortunately, the post-war goal has been a very good one for them: economic prosperity. But if you switch that direction?

RC: You know, Bernie, with all due respect to Chie Nakane, whom I do respect a lot, I wrote a piece last year about *The Chrysanthemum and the Sword* for *The Wall Street Journal* in which I said anthropology—and I think it's true of sociology as well—is a descriptive science. It's like a camera. You take a picture, and you've got that image right. But you can't extrapolate from that and say here's what this society is going to be like twenty years from now, because, if you look at Ruth Benedict's book, it becomes very apparent that she hadn't a clue what Japan was going to be like twenty years from now.

In fact, insofar as she makes any predictions at all, they're dead wrong. I don't think you can say, "this society is like this, and so in the future, they're always gonna behave that way." Japanese society is changing. For one thing, I think they're a less driven people now. And they're probably going to be progressively less driven.

BK: Who are some of the Japanese whom you admire the most, either living or dead?

RC: I admired Shigeru Yoshida a lot, whom I thought was a very skillful manipulator, in very difficult times. I have enormous respect for Yoshiya Ariyoshi, the late chairman of NYK, who I think was, for a man brought up when he was, extraordinarily cosmopolitan and far-sighted. I respect Chie Nakane a lot, although I don't always agree with her. In terms of obscure people, there's a fellow at MITI, Naito Masahisa, who I think is just one of the smartest people I've known, sort of symptomatic of what I was talking about, about this new sophistication and cosmopolitanism, yet he's very Japanese.

Among politicians, I think (ex-Prime Minister Yasuhiro) Nakasone is a very hopeful person, in the sense that he's probably the first Japanese prime minister in my lifetime, or since Yoshida, who could deal easily with the outside world. I don't know, I'm not given to having heroes, so I'll tell you somebody I really respect, and that's a woman named Kawaguchi Yoriko who works at MITI and who is handling a very difficult situation with tremendous skill and grace. I think she could well be the first Japanese woman to really make it big in the bureaucracy. I liked Yukio Mishima. He was bright and fascinating. And he had style; God knows, he had style.

BK: What about the people you didn't like? Any Japanese you don't like?

RC: Yes, but there is nobody very important that I ever had a real dislike for whom I can think of offhand. I'm not sure I should even mention it, but there was a professor, a writer who symbolized that class of career Japanese intellectuals, who mostly drive me up the wall. They're so damn satisfied with themselves, and convinced that they've got clean hands. They would never think of "meddling," if you will, with politics in this country. These intellectuals feel they are all much too moral to get involved in it.

BK: What do you find disagreeable about Japan? Any disturbing experiences?

RC: None of a major kind but a lot of little ones. There's a certain kind of arrogance. For example, recently, when I was getting ready to make a speech in Osaka, they brought in the interpreters, and I told one of them I'm going to make some changes. And he said, "well, I would assume so—you're not going to read this, are you?" And I replied, "well, that's why I gave you the text. Yes, I'll probably make some changes, but I'm gonna read it." And he said: "Oh, it's going to take you an hour and a half to read this." He was just putting me down, all along the line. Trying to show, somehow, that he was an expert and I an amateur. It was a certain kind of arrogance that I've encountered occasionally from clerks, office people, customs inspectors, which I really don't like at all. People who are trying to show that they're a little better than you are, a little smarter— whatever.

BK: Have you ever been deceived?

RC: Oh no, but if I have any single complaint it's that on occasion people have expected more of me than I thought they were entitled to. They would presume on relatively brief acquaintance, that they were entitled to make demands on me which I didn't feel they were entitled to. And that's happened fairly frequently. And when I can't deliver what they expect they react with great indignation. They act as though I had betrayed them.

I'll tell you a story, a private story.

Somebody I know reasonably well in Japan came to the States, and, at my instigation, actually, he wanted to rent a car, and I said fine, I'll arrange for that, but I'll need your licence. He said, he didn't have a licence not even a Japanese licence. In that case I said, "I'm awfully sorry, but without a licence, you can't rent a car." He said, "can't you talk to them? Can't we talk to the police?" I said "no."

He must have thought he was in Southeast Asia or in the Middle East. He was very annoyed with me. He thought that I was just not willing to go to the trouble on his behalf, but I thought it was really incredible that he would expect this.

That's an extreme case.

But there have been a number of cases where people have sort of implied that I really owe them on obligation, when I didn't; I couldn't see that I did. But nobody's ever done anything that I felt was really cruel or vicious to me. It's been more just sort of minor social irritations.

BK: Have we left out anything?

RC: Just one thing. I regret that I've never lived here for a long period. By coming in and out, I do notice changes that perhaps if I had been here all along, I wouldn't have noticed so much.

And this is a question as well as a point I noticed the other day I was coming in from Narita and I took a taxi. We went through a toll booth and the guy got the slip, right? We drove about two or three hundred yards on down the thru-way, and the driver crumpled it up and threw it out the window, the way Americans do. You got something you don't want, you throw it out the window! That struck me; I mean, it drives everybody where I live in Connecticut crazy, because these twenty-year-old kids drive around, and throw everything out the window of their car, and it requires a major clean-up effort to keep the town from looking like somebody's garbage. And I would think, well, that doesn't happen in Japan—but it's beginning to.

Japan as We Lived It

Bernard Krisher

"Tokyo is the most exciting city in the world."

Japan as We Lived It

Mary Lord[*]: Wearing a blue suit and a loud tie, Mr. Krisher sat for his first interview with the Western press. How does it feel to be on the other side of the interview for a change?

Bernard Krisher: Fun.

ML: Well, let's start with the obvious question.

When people hear, oh, you're going to Japan, everyone says, look up Mr. Krisher. After more than twenty-three years here, you have become, in the eyes of many Americans, Mr. Japan, and you have a coterie of devoted followers. How do you trace your evolution? What were you like when you first came here? What prompted you to come here? How have your impressions of Japan changed over the course of more than two decades, if they have at all?

BK: That answer should take about two hours. But let's start from the beginning. I came to Japan by accident, I was a reporter for the *New York World Telegram and Sun* and I asked my boss, the city editor, for a raise. In lieu of a raise he took out a letter from his desk and he said, "How'd you like to take a trip to Europe? We've just received an invitation from the Pentagon for a reporter to visit European bases for five or six weeks."

ML: Probably an exercise or something?

BK: No, in those days they were very generous with junkets; they invited journalists. I had been at the other end of this when I had been in the Army in Germany from 1953 to '55 in the Public Information Division in Heidelberg. I used to escort journalists like that. And so, for the Brooklyn section of the *World Telegram and Sun* I spent five or six weeks in Europe in 1957, visiting various countries and bases, writing about the GIs from Brooklyn along the German-Czech border and other such exotic assignments. That series was quite successful and, the following year,

---

[*]Mary Lord, ex-Newsweek/Washington correspondent, is the Tokyo bureau chief for U.S. News and World Report and is now its business editor, based in Washington.

1958, the Pentagon wrote again and said: we liked your series last year, how would you like to follow up and do a similar series in Asia. I went back to the city editor and I took this second trip out to the Far East—Japan, Korea, Okinawa, Hong Kong, the Philippines, Taiwan—a fantastic discovery for someone in his early twenties. And I fell in love with Japan.

I had read Lafcadio Hearn, Michener's *Sayonara,* and, mixed with my own observations, it was a world so different and interesting, and romantic; it was something I really wanted to get into. And so, when I returned to the States, I decided to take a couple of evening courses at Columbia, applied for a Ford Foundation fellowship for Advanced International Reporting, also at Columbia, was accepted, and spent the next fifteen months studying at the East Asian Institute, cramming intensive Japanese, on a leave of absence from the *Telegram.* The *Telegram* at one point, however asked me to come back and not pursue this any further because there was really no purpose knowing all that much about one country for a local paper like the *World Telegram.*

ML: Because they couldn't figure out how many Brooklyn boys would ever be passing through there that would make it worthwhile?

BK: Exactly. So I quit the *World Telegram* and applied to various publications, *The New York Times, Washington Post,Newsweek,Time,* AP, UPI, and asked them if there was a position in Japan. Many offered me positions with their organizations but no guarantee that I would get to Japan. *Newsweek* and UPI, however said that if I happened to get to Japan on my own steam, they'd be happy to send a note to their local bureau chief and that might result in a local stringer job. So I decided to go with that.

ML: You had no guarantee at all?

BK: No, I just came out here and I went to see Ernie Hoberecht of UPI, and Ray Steinberg, the *Newsweek* bureau chief. Hoberecht offered me $50 a week to work for

UPI and Steinberg offered me $60 a week because he didn't like Hoberecht. Steinberg also clinched the deal for me when he said, "You'll learn lots more at *Newsweek* than at UPI where you'd be sitting six days a week in some boiler room, rewriting copy. With *Newsweek,* you'll meet five or six new people a week; you'll have a collection of *meishi* and some day you'll really know your way around Japan." So I took the Steinberg offer but Steinberg shortly thereafter got into a fight with Arnaud de Borchgrave, who was foreign editor, and quit. Ruri Kawashima, the editorial assistant, who is now the program director of the Japan Society, and I held the fort for about nine months without title or rank, but we ran the bureau. Then a bureau chief, James Truitt, came out for three years and I became a fully fledged correspondent, and when Truitt left in 1967, I became bureau chief and that's how I got to be here and stayed here. I stuck with *Newsweek* until 1980.

ML: If you had been a little bit older or wiser, would you have taken that original dare? It must have taken a lot of courage to leave a secure job at a reputable news organization.

BK: Definitely, but I always wanted to be a foreign correspondent, since I was in high school. I was also a little unhappy with American journalism; that is, with working on a daily newspaper in the United States, because as the union, the Newspaper Guild, became stronger—which is good on the one hand, because newspaper people shouldn't be exploited—the papers became more economically oriented and they began to cut down on coverage.

There was less and less outside coverage and more dependency on press agents and wire stuff; there was a lot of rewriting in the office which somehow didn't appeal to me anymore. I wanted to go out, touch the flesh and report. And I also felt Americans should be better informed about the world beyond America. If democracy is to work better, the public should know what is happening abroad and what the US is doing overseas. As so much US tax money is spent on foreign countries and so many foreign policy decisions are made by people in Washington on matters the public knows very little about, I saw it as a mission, too, to be out there and check on what's going on.

ML: I guess journalists really should be, in part, missionaries. We would make good teachers, good ministers.

BK: Part missionary, part educator and, also, you can become an expert once you've been working on something long enough.

ML: Do you remember, just to backtrack a bit, what your first impression was? Do you remember any one particular incident or place or person that at that moment told you, yes, I want to come back here to live?

BK: Well the fact that everything was so different, and it worked! I wanted to find out why people looked so different, acted so differently. Especially in 1958, everything was so totally different in this country.

ML: No buildings of any size probably?

BK: Well, downtown there were buildings but none of these skyscrapers. There was the Dai-Ichi and some of those other buildings along the Palace moat. That was the skyline.

ML: No *gaijin* ghettos like Roppongi?

BK: Well foreigners always seemed to gather in Roppongi, maybe because of its proximity to the military compounds—Washington Heights, Hardy Barracks, the Stars and Stripes. But there was no Okura Hotel or Kasumigaseki Building.

ML: Hard to imagine.

BK: But the Hamburger Inn was there.

ML: It must have been a very small and elite community of Westerners at that time?

BK: Well, it was the end of the military period. I stayed at the Sanno Hotel in 1958.

ML: Did you find it hard to work here? Was the language a problem, did you find that you could scratch the surface and then not get beyond?

Japan as We Lived It

BK: Well, at the very beginning there was a considerable period where I wasn't really sure whether what I was reporting was really the truth. It was hard. You guessed, you surmised, you talked to people but you couldn't get to the bottom.

The Japanese people also were not very good analysts of their own society. They gave you a few facts. But you couldn't get anything unless you met them personally. And it usually required several meetings before someone felt comfortable talking to you.

Nowadays you can do a lot by telephone but in those days everything had to be done personally, even checking or rechecking a fact or just asking one question. People wanted to meet you, look at you. So it took three or four times as long to do a story. Nothing could be done over the telephone.

ML: Is that because they were afraid of secrets or was it just the custom?

BK: The custom. Now that Japan has become a busier society, the mechanics of reporting, thank God, have also speeded up. Now when I want to call on people, people say "Why don't we do it by phone?" I remember my first shock when Akio Morita, the chairman of Sony, whom I used to meet frequently in those days, suddenly one day, when I asked for an appointment, said, "What do you want to talk about? Can you ask me the question right now over the phone?" And we settled the whole thing in 10 minutes over the phone. I think I was in a shock for a day because I never imagined this would be possible in Japan.

ML: Probably it took ten years to get to that point.

BK: Yes. But what really bothered me as a journalist were the barriers to people. Some sources just wouldn't meet you without a proper introduction. Introductions are very important in Japan. In those days people also didn't know what *Newsweek* was, so you had to explain.

Still, many Japanese felt no reason really to see you; you're a foreigner, they didn't know you, they didn't know your magazine, and, furthermore, politicians saw little value appearing in such a magazine; it wouldn't get them re-elected.

I remember when President Kennedy was assassinated and *Newsweek* wanted to know what the prime minister had done that day and what his reaction had been, I called the prime minister's secretary, Mr. Kuroda, who is now ambassador to the United Nations. I remember all these things vividly. I asked him about how Mr. Ikeda reacted when he heard the news and he said he was very sorry but, since I was not a member of the press club,

I couldn't get any information from the prime minister's office.

I got quite hysterical. I said: "Our president, the president of the United States, has just been assassinated! Japan is an ally of the United States; my company has sent me here to report about Japan. You are such a closed society, your government is so closed"—I was really furious—"you won't even comment about the death of our president to a reporter for the American people!" and I just hung up the phone. And then, five minutes later, the *kanji* of the prime minister's office, his name was also Mr. Ikeda, Kanjo Ikeda, called me back. He was the *Asahi Shimbun* correspondent and also head of the press club for the month; he said: "Mr. Krisher I understand that you just called Mr. Kuroda and wanted to get some information about what the prime minister did this morning, this is what the prime minister did. And this is what he thinks."

ML: Unheard of in America for the press to tell each other things like that.

BK: That's the system in Japan, the prime minister is totally under the control of the press that covers him. And his agreement or the general agreement between sources and the press is to deal only with the group of reporters who cover them. These are the infamous Japanese press clubs. In this case, I could only get my information by dealing with the press club, getting my news through another reporter, which is something I would not have done in the United

States—it just isn't proper, you do your own reporting, you don't ask another reporter to be the intermediary for news.

The point is that this country can be covered and can be conquered business-wise and 'other-wise' if you are willing to learn and study and go through their sort of incongruous system. In the end you don't lose, because no one is supposed to be pushed into a corner. My anger made Mr. Kuroda so uncomfortable, I suppose, that he couldn't ignore it. So he went to the press club and begged them to call me. Special case.

ML: Well that's an interesting case. Is your success somewhat attributable to the fact that you see the system and either pretend not to understand it when it doesn't work to your advantage or to fight against it?

BK: Well I fought against the system here. Sometimes it was with a carrot and sometimes with a stick. But I was always fighting one way or another. I never totally accepted it.

As an American journalist, during the time when I was working for *Newsweek* and then *Fortune*, I felt that I should basically be an American correspondent and cover news, or have the gut reactions and feelings of an American journalist. Sometimes in the strategy and the means of making contacts and eliciting news from sources, you have to do it in the manner that is familiar to the people you're dealing with. But, yes, I continuously considered, I still consider, public officials to be crooks, whether they're American or Japanese. Not that they necessarily are.

ML: That's a skeptical attitude.

BK: Yes. There are many things about the system that I didn't like and still don't like; on balance, however, if I'm asked about Japan, I find, in general, that there are enough good things which balance the bad ones. For everything I don't like about the system there are so many things that I do like.

ML: Like high prices....But you do get after-care service.

BK: Exactly. Or, the society is very conformist, dull in some ways, but it's safe and people are polite and friendships stick. When you make a friend you have him forever; long relationships do hold. Mr. Kanjo Ikeda, of the *Asahi*, subsequently became a very good friend and he took me along on an election campaign trip of then-Prime Minister Hayato Ikeda. No foreign journalist had ever been on such a trip. It was most revealing. Kanjo died a few years ago and I really miss him. The society, however, is changing in small degrees. People are not as conscientious anymore; they're getting a bit more pragmatic.

ML: Is that a result of modernization or have they been taught the hard way by the rest of the world?

BK: I think it's economics probably. You can't afford the luxury any more of long travel to meet somebody. Salaries have tripled, a newspaper company can no longer afford to send a reporter out to meet someone just for one fact; to go somewhere for a whole day to come back with one fact. Run up all the gas, driver and so on. So things have become more compact.

ML: Well you also told me some very interesting stories about *geisha* parties. Your first days as a foreign correspondent seem rather exotic compared to now. You used to go to one once a week in the old days.

BK: Exactly. To three the first week when I came to Japan. I had introductions to a number of people and they immediately took me to *geisha* parties. Nowadays they take you to a coffee shop. There seems to be an inverse relationship between a country's economy and the quality of its entertainment; the more beautiful the girls in the bars and in the *geisha* houses, the poorer the economy. In Korea you still find the most beautiful women in the clubs and *kiseng* houses, but that's declining too, as the economy is prospering.

ML: Now they're all office ladies?

BK: Right.

ML: Do you think there is more of an attitude that the

foreign press is something to be courted, rather than just dealt with?

BK: I don't think the foreign press is that much appreciated, or regarded as so important. It took Prime Minister Nakasone almost four years before he accepted an invitation to speak at the Foreign Correspondents Club.

Perhaps certain corners of Japan, like the Japan National Tourist Orgainzation or the computer companies, for whom the foreign press at this particular point may be useful or valuable, will go out of their way and set aside some budget to cooperate with inquiries from the foreign press, but the Japanese like to do things according to their schedule.

When they decide to invite a group of correspondents to their plant and give them a nice luxurious weekend and shower gifts on them, that's when they want you to be there and they're unhappy when you're not. They have their once-a-year great party, or function, or buffet and they make an all out effort to get a large turnout. But the rest of the year, if you happen to call them, you're a nuisance; if you want to visit their plant, it doesn't fit into their schedule; everybody is too busy to meet you. They are also hesitant to make appointments for you with their top executives for fear the executive may suddenly be busy or called away and that would mean a cancellation. They hate to cancel things for foreigners.

ML: So you changed more than you succeeded in changing the system, I'm afraid.

BK: Well, you adapt, but also, if you have been here a long time and if you represent an organization that's important to them, you can dictate a few things yourself. I mean you can call a company or some government official or even the prime minister and push to get an interview. And if you push hard enough and throw in a few arguments to persuade them of the value of seeing you, they will see you but its not so easy; you can't just pick up the phone and say you want to see somebody.

ML: You're somewhat of a celebrity for having interviewed the emperor; would you consider that your greatest triumph?

BK: Yes, I think it's the greatest, the most difficult feat and probably the thing that I treasure most.

ML: How long was it in preparation?

BK: Well, you could divide it in two periods; one started the day I landed in Japan. It was already in my mind then to interview the Emperor.

ML: And everyone of course said it couldn't be done.

BK: Yes, I didn't actively pursue it until much later. What I really wanted to prove was that I knew when and how to succeed. So, first of all, timing was important. I would have to have a reason for interviewing him and there was only one good one. It would come the day of the announcement that he would visit the United States. That was nine months off. It would be an occasion which would make a reason why I, Bernie Krisher, bureau chief of *Newsweek*, a major American magazine, was requesting an interview, to introduce him to the American public. So, that't where I began, nine months before that day.

ML: Prior to that you really hadn't written any stories about the imperial family?

BK: Oh yes, indirect stories; I wrote a story when Prince Hironomiya entered kindergarten at Gakushuin. I interviewed his kindergarten teacher. And I did a story on that. And then I did a story which subsequently hurt me in trying to get the interview with the emperor. That was a story on Mr. Usami, the chief chamberlain of the Imperial Household Agency. I called him the "emperor's keeper" and "the shadow emperor", the man who makes decisions behind the scenes. And sort of depicted him as...

ML: Mr. "Eminence Grise."

BK: Right, in the process of asking for the interview that posed a problem. What I was doing during those nine months was consensus building and a rather high degree of consensus had been reached.

ML: With everyone who could possibly be of help.

BK: That's right; asking them not necessarily to help me but not to oppose the project if it ever came to them to voice an opinion. And my request suddenly reached the Imperial Houshold Agency and Mr. Usami was in the delicate position of making the decision of refusing me without making it appear that he was refusing me because I had done the article on him.

ML: Maybe it worked to your advantage.

BK: Well, he couldn't bring that up as a reason but he brought up other reasons.

ML: So you were refused?

BK: No, not directly. I heard it indirectly.

ML: How did you go about to build the consensus?

BK: Well, what I did was basically this: I thought it was important to do three things. One, to convince the Japanese government that my request should be considered to have some value: a good interview with the emperor prior to his departure, preparatory to the trip, would help the trip, to make it a success, that was everyone's goal. I tried to persuade them that my interview in *Newsweek* would contribute to that. I therefore aimed to talk to enough people who would be consulted, as no one in this country has the power to decide something like that by himself.

I wasn't a head of state nor a prime minister; I was someone who suddenly came out of the blue and wanted to see the emperor who had never met anyone like me—Japanese or foreigner—on a one-to-one basis. I wanted everyone in the bureaucracy not to oppose it. I met close to one hundred people during that period, for lunch or at their offices, in the foreign ministry, the prime ministter's office, secretaries and ministers, and so on, and I said to them "I know that you can't actively pursue this"—in fact it was dangerous for people to push it, it might hurt their careers— "but, if it ever comes before you, please don't oppose it." I got everyone to agree to that except one person. Oddly enough, he was the same Mr. Kuroda, once Prime Minister Hayato Ikeda's secretary, who was now head of the public information division of the Foreign Ministry. He was furious with me for even suggesting something like that, being a real royalist. "Who do you think you are?" he asked me.

ML: You commoner.

BK: I think it hurt him later. I believe he was not assigned to be the public relations official on the emperor's trip because he seemed too inflexible. Anyway that was that.

And the third thing I asked everybody was to keep it secret, not to discuss my proposal, because I didn't want anyone else to sabotage it or stymie it, particularly the Japanese press, who surely would oppose it, or the other foreign correspondents who might then also demand such an interview. If there were too many requests there could be no exclusive interview. So, nobody else asked. I seemed to be the only one doggedly pursuing an interview with the emperor.

After I felt I had amassed my consensus, I went out and met most of the Cabinet ministers—Mr. Riichi Miyazawa, who was foreign minister, Mr. Takeo Fukuda, who was finance minister and who was delegated to accompany the emperor on his trip, the chief cabinet secretary, Mr. Ide, who had the most power as the liaison with the Imperial Household Agency, and the secretary to the prime minister, Mr. Takeo Miki. It looked pretty good and then there was a long summer wait. This was June and I was supposed to wait until July, August. I went up to Yamanakaka for a month. Just waiting. They said they would let me know at the end of August. In the meantime, word got back to me that the Imperial Household Agency was opposing the proposal, they didn't want any exclusive interview. Instead they wanted a series of interviews or a group session. There was a group session after my interview.

For a moment, if looked like it had all fallen apart. Internally they were asking, why *Newsweek*? *Time* had more circulation and the *New York Times* was more prestigious. They were right on both counts so I had to find a way to "sell" *Newsweek*. I argued that I had been here longer, a news magazine was available all week, while a newspaper was only on sale for one day; the *New York Times* doesn't circulate in other cities, so it would be unfair to the newspapers in Chicago or Los Angeles; *Newsweek* is national. And also I had been reporting from Japan for more than a decade. *Time* had just had a change of bureau chiefs. Ed Reingold had just left or was about to leave and somebody else was coming or had come and this man had no Japan experience.

ML: Incredible. It must have taken a lot of *nemawashi*, a lot of the binding of the roots.

BK: Well, the Imperial Household Agency finally agreed; okay, *Newsweek* is fine but we'd rather have the editor of *Newsweek* come out, not the correspondent in Tokyo. They were thinking of inviting Oz Elliott or someone on a higher level. I told the foreign minister if that was the case then I would ask to leave Japan. There was no reason for me to have spent all these years in Japan, covering this country, you know, and then get that type of rub-off. They said no, no Mr. Krisher, you're a very valuable treasure of Japan, we don't want you to do that—we'll have to see about that. And then finally ....

ML: That was a better story than the interview itself.

BK: But I had not overcome all hurdles yet; there was still Mr. Usami himself. He still opposed my being the interviewer. So I researched and found who was close enough to persuade him to change his mind. I discovered that Mr. Toshio Kimura, a former foreign minister whom I knew, was his cousin. I went to see him and asked if he could personally talk to Mr. Usami on my behalf. He promised to do that but said he couldn't do it immediately, only if an occasion presented itself where he coincidentally met Mr. Usami, and that didn't happen more than once or twice a month. We would have to wait for that. The day that he coincidentally met him he called me and said he had passed on the word.

And then there was another person, the son of the master of ceremonies at the palace, whom I knew well, and he asked his father to put in a good word. That clinched the deal, I think.

ML: Incredible. And the entire interview was 20 minutes?

BK: 32 Minutes.

ML: And no one's ever done it since?

BK: Well, yes and no. there were a few other short meetings after mine, ten-minute handshakes and things like that. The key thing that made this an interview, actually, was the fact that at the last moment they got cold feet, they didn't really want an exclusive interview. So they suggested that I bring my wife along, and the empress would also be there. It would be a meeting of the Krishers and the emperor and empress. Akiko, my Japanese wife, was wise enough, and sacrificial enough, to refuse. What Japanese would ever refuse such an invitation? She said "No, it's a trick, they want to make it a social occasion and rob you of the opportunity of an interview; this is your job and this is your work, and, if I'm not there, then it will be a real interview, which he's never had before." So I relayed that she couldn't or wouldn't make it. And then I got my one-to-one interview.

ML: Fantastic. What do you consider your biggest disappointment? The thing you really screwed up most and regretted later?

BK: I've never regretted anything. I think everything you do in life has a value. But my greatest disappointment in Japan or with the Japanese was their treatment of the Vietnamese. That gave me a whole new perspective on Japan. I had always been quite sympathetic to Japan; one has to be sympathetic to a culture, not necessarily to the government, or to the politics of the country, but you cannot report or be close to something unless you have some feeling for it. I mean, if you're a scientist, you have to be interested in science, etc.. So, I've always liked, admired Japanese society and culture, their sense of beauty and harmony, the way they reach consensus, Japanese-type democracy, many things. But I never really saw the sub-cultural "black spots," or gave much thought to them. But when the Vietnam War ended and when all the boat people were looking around for a haven elsewhere, and countries as small as Switzerland, all the way in Europe, took in Vietnamese. The Swedes, the French, the Americans, the Germans, people so distant and so culturally and racially apart from the Vietnamese, all opened their doors to the refugees, I suddenly realized how selfish the Japanese could be. The Japanese just refused. The refugees couldn't come into Japan. Not only Japanese boats but also foreign boats couldn't land in Japan if they had Vietnamese refugees on them. The Japanese authorities wouldn't let these people off the boat. That got me so upset. The arguments that were raised at that time were, these people would never fit in; they didn't speak the language; the Japanese people would never accept them; they don't even want to stay here if you ask them— you know, every excuse or pretext. So I wrote a piece in *Newsweek*, a bylined piece about this, saying nothing had ever disappointed me as much about the Japanese as their treatment of the Vietnamese. You could really detect their xenophobia, that they'd never been part of the world. Actually my criticism was really directed against the government, because I knew, like the textbook issue or fingerprinting of aliens, this was just an outdated stubborn bureaucratic policy and didn't reflect Japanese public opinion. And my article apparently had a big impact here. Many of the newspapers picked it up and the *Asahi Shimbun* even ran almost a whole page feature on the subject, featuring an interview with me.

ML: The star witness for the prosecution?

BK: And I think that embarrassed the Japanese. Even the American embassy people said "Go slow on them," or something like that, "don't hit them too hard; eventually they'll adjust their policy. You have to give them time."

ML: I'm amazed that the embassy people did say that.

BK: They didn't like the Japanese to be hit. There's a very soft group here at the embassy. Maybe some of the old-timers, the Occupation types who felt we had pushed the Japanese into too much. There had been a lot of pushing during the Occupation and probably some Americans felt any harsh criticism was a throw back to that era. But the article did have an impact.

ML: But then they took in what? Two refugees or so as I remember?

BK: Two or three, symbolically, but later they got pretty credible on the subject. They were not bringing in thousands but they came up with a system. Vietnamese and Cambodians can settle in this country now and become permanent citizens, and they get quite a bit of attention, actually, to make sure that they settle in. At first, you know, the Salvation Army and the Red Cross kept them, but now it's a government program, which is quite unique for Japan. I mean, this is basically a country that has never permitted foreign workers, migrant workers here. If I contributed to softening their stand towards the Vietnamese refugees, that's also one of my big accomplishments. I do credit myself, I think, with having to some degree pushed that change because even people from the Foreign Ministry came to visit me at *Newsweek,* to try to get me to "understand" their position. I recall the people who came, telling me, "we're trying; we're doing this and that." And I said, "it's not enough!"

ML: What other successes or disappointment?

BK: Probably the other, the third thing which I indirectly, and not with malice, may be slightly responsible for, is the Tanaka resignation. It all started with a *Bungei Shinju* article about Mr. Tanaka's corruption and women problems which normally would have died out in Japan because a magazine article usually is not picked up by the press. It dies a natural death.

However, this case was different. A Japanese businessman, who was the *Newsweek* bureau's neighbor in our Ginza office, tipped me off that *Bungei Shunju* would be running this long article in about two weeks. I persuaded the magazine's editor, another Mr. Tanaka, to let me see the galleys of the Tachibana article before publication and I had a member of my staff translate it. I then filed a story on the article and its sigificance which ran in *Newsweek* one day after *Bungei Shunju* appeared.

The *Baltimore Sun* correspondent then asked me whether this appeared only in the international or also in the domestic edition? I said only international. He said, "Oh. great! Then I can introduce it in America." And I gave him my notes and the translated text of the *Bungei Shinju* article.

And so he ran it on a Wednesday. The *Washington Post* foreign editor, Phil Foisie saw it and called up his Tokyo correspondent Don Oberdorfer, who shared an office with me. I had, in fact told Oberdorfer about my picking up the story, but he was uninterested. Now, however, he seemed quite excited and said, "Can I see your notes?" So he wrote the same story again the next day. And it ran on the front page of the *Washington Post*, Friday.

So, *Bungei Shinju* came out on a Monday; we had the story in *Newsweek* on Tuesday (because I had obtained the advanced galleys), the *Baltimore Sun* came out on Wednesday and the *Post* Friday on the front page. The *Yomiuri Shimbun* then played it back from Washington, saying first *Newsweek* then the *Baltimore Sun*, now the *Washington* on the front page.

This was the way the *Bungei Shinju* article survived and became a topic in the Japanese press—via the foreign press.

Then Tanaka refused to have any press conferences after that. But he had been scheduled to speak at the Foreign Correspondents Club the following Tuesday. He wanted to cancel that appearance but was advised by his secretary, Mr. Kiuchi, that the foreign press were 'gentlemen' and would not embarass him. The press conference had also been scheduled a long time ago because Tanaka was about to leave the following week for New Zealand and Australia. All the questions, he was told by his staff, would be about his trip, "So don't worry, Mr. Tanaka." And then he was introduced by the acting club president, Bela Elias, the vice president, who was a Hungarian, and who started out by quoting the *Newsweek* story.

He said: "You've all probably read the *Newsweek* story about Mr. Tanaka—what are your questions?"

And then question one, two, three, four and five were about Lockheed, "the corruption," and all that. Tanaka got furious and just walked out of the Press Club in mid-interview. That made front page news the next day in the Japanese press, and it was the beginning of the end.

ML: So much for 'you gentlemen of the press.'

BK: Newsweek may have been the fuse that caused the fire.

ML: Did you and *Newsweek* always see eye to eye?

BK: Newsweek saw its golden days under the helm of Osborn Elliott, now the dean of Columbia University's Graduate School of Journalism. He was an outstanding editor; he revitalized *Newsweek* and made it one of the great American magazines. He was backed by such talented editors as Kermit Lansner and Robert Christopher—all of whom were eventually eased out by Newsweek's mercurial owner, Katherine Graham.

ML: Who are the most interesting people, or types, that you've met in Japan?

BK: Well, they really range. The emperor, certainly, is a very interesting person. He was very economical with words. He had a great sense of duty. I think he knows his role exactly. And, given his personality, he's probably a man who does his job to perfection. I would give him a very high quality control rating—over what he has been programmed to do. He has handled himself without ever, I think, faltering from his assigned role. And my interview with him was certainly very memorable.

At the other end of the scale are some of the Yakuza, a Mr. Sasaki of the Yamaguchigumi, Mr. Inagawa, who is in Atami, whom I interviewed once, and who totally undressed for me to show me his body etched with tattoos—right smack in the midst of our interview! I still have pictures.

ML: And you didn't even have to push, right?

BK: A lot of doors opened like that just because I was a foreigner. I said "tatoos?" And he said, "yes." And I asked, "where?" and he said, "all over!" and then he totally undressed! With Ruri Kawashima in the room!

And, oh, Mr. Yoshiya Ariyoshi, who was the chairman of NYK, a wonderful, wonderful man, very internationally-oriented, and very kind. He used to send my son, Joseph, postcards from all over the world with hotel pictures on them, because Joseph collected hotel postcards. Mr. Ariyoshi was, in my view, the "youngest" and most-internationalized Japanese.

Chie Nakane and Takeo Doi gave me great insights into Japan. Chie Nakane talked about the fact that the Japanese have no principles, that everything is done case by case. That was a great insight, which also made the Vietnamese refugee situation understandable. I learned the Japanese don't act but they react.

I also retain an impression of Yukio Mishima, who always tried to explain suicide to me, and of Yasunari Kawabata, who took about five minutes to answer every question. And Tetsuzo Fuwa, the head of the Communist Party, who acted very much like a Japanese business executive. In fact, the thing that impressed me generally about the Japanese was how similar they really are. In most other countries, you would say a French journalist, for examples, was more similar to an American journalist than to another Frenchman. But in Japan the culture is so strong that a Japanese Communist, for example, is not so different from a Japanese businessmen, or even from a member of the United Red Army.

ML: In what way?

BK: They have the same relationships within the organization. The pattern of behavior is very similar, whether it's among radical terrorists, punk freaks, Communists, or businessmen. The way they relate to the people who work with them, their associates, enemies and so on; the degree of politeness, the way they interact, obligations, etc. It's like the *sumo* game. Everybody starts by throwing salt, bowing. Those cultural rituals are very strong, whatever it is that they have to do. All hell can break loose but at the end it's back to the ritual. Like the exit of a discredited official or politician: it's not a sharp, quick demise; everyone is usually allowed his *hanamichi*.

ML: What about places? The most interesting places in Japan?

BK: In the early years I used to travel constantly throughout Japan. A city I found most memorable was certainly Kurashiki. I liked it very much because it still has some old converted warehouses and stables. I felt a great sense of discovery when I saw it. We took a trip in a Volkswagen there in 1964—just before the Olympics, even before the highway was completed. We drove from Tokyo to Kagoshima in two weeks. One week to get down there and one week to get back. Every night around five or six we would stop wherever we happened to be. And we hit upon Kurashiki by accident, not knowing it even existed or what it was. And going into the Kurashiki Kokusai Hotel and finding a giant *Munakata* woodblock print right there in the lobby, plus the good service; it was just splendid. And the museums—the Van Goghs and the Renoirs, in this small little museum right there in the rice paddies.

Then Hida Takayama, which is, I think, nicer than Kyoto in many ways, a charming, ancient town. And Hagi, where many of Meiji leaders came from. And an island called Hekurajima, which is way out, off Kanazawa. You had to take a three-hour boat trip and you couldn't stay there overnight because there were no hotels. Maybe there's an inn now but there wasn't then. I stayed with a farm family. That's where naked women divers still dive for abalone.

ML: That's why you probably went there!

BK: Of course, Foscoe Maraini the Italian writer, wrote a marvelous book about Hekurajima. I did a story on baths once. I went all the way from Noboribetsu, on the tip of Hokkaido, down to Ibusiki, which is at the bottom of Kyushu, just to write about mixed bathing.

And, of course, I like Tokyo. I think Tokyo is the most exciting city in the world.

ML: Why?

BK: Because it's alive; people are happy; it is, in a sense, what New York once was. I still love New York, I mean, it's my city, and so much is still great, but, when a city once had a peak and isn't as great as it once was, there's somehow some disappointment, right?

ML: Bloom off the rose.

BK: But Tokyo right now is at its height; so much is going on here. And I think many foreigners are also contributing to Tokyo, creatively and in many other ways.

ML: I've noticed that, too. The internationalized Japanese have done much to open their country up to the rest of the world and, also, in a sense, to their fellow Japanese. They go to Europe and bring fashion back; they go to America, create there and also bring art back.

BK: There's lots of that; people do want to come here, to do things in Japan. It looks good for them, too. Isaac Stern and Madonna do concerts in Tokyo and I think they get a special kick out of that. They seem prouder of it than if they went to Paris or London. If they perform in Tokyo, they'll bring a poster back with some Japanese writing on it and hang it in their studio!

ML: Do you think you could ever go back and live in America or are you pretty tied to Japan?

BK: I think I can do either. I usually feel the center is where I am. That sounds very egocentric but I think I can adjust or work or start up anywhere again. Maybe I'm like an aging boxer who still thinks he can win a prize fight. Maybe it's more difficult to just move and start fresh. But, mentally, I'm prepared for anything. Basically what keeps me here is the fact that I've made many connections, I operate well. I have a secure income, a good job as chief editorial advisor to *FOCUS* magazine, the most successful and largest circulating weekly in Japan, which I helped to develop at Shinchosha, and I think I'm otherwise also contributing something original and productive to this society and to US-Japan relations. I can do more where I'm presently located. But if I had something interesting in New York or in Washington—I think I'd always have to be in a big city—I don't see why I couldn't live there. I'm not a permanent expatriate. I don't want to die in Japan.

ML: How do you rate the vision of Tokyo on the outside world with the vision of Japan on the outside world?

BK: Differently in different places. And totally inaccurate, in most cases. In Europe, they don't know very much about Japan. On a trip to Europe last summer, I visited many editors and journalists, intelligent people, some of whom had not been to Japan. Their image was so distorted. They wondered what I saw in Japan, how could I stay there for more than twenty years, how could I stand it. They marveled how I could "deal" with those people. I didn't want to say that I could not ever see myself living more than a couple of years—at most—in France, Germany, Italy or even England. But I could live in Japan for two or three decades and be very happy.

The view from Japan toward the outside world is much clearer, yet I wonder why, with so many Japanese who have actually been overseas and have seen how people live there, that there is not more of a movement here to demand better housing, lower prices for consumer goods and generally a higher quality of life. When you talk about trade imbalance and all those injustices, the Japanese are not really the beneficiaries of all that revenue. Look at the life of the people who produce all these remarkable products that flood the world. They may be producing and selling all that stuff but whom does it benefit? What can people really buy with their salaries? How much time do they have to spend with their families? How big are their homes? How many vacation days do they have? How warm are their living rooms? It's all at the bottom of the scale. Much below a middle-income family, not only in the US, France, Italy, but also Singapore, Manila—even Indonesia.

I think, middle class Indonesians, or the urban middle class in other Asian countries, have much more space. An Indonesian could never live in the space a Japanese lives in. Or commute that long. I don't think most Indonesians, even the poorest Indonesian, would trade places with an average salary man in Japan. It's not in the culture in those countries to sacrifice that much. Even in pre-war Japan, I think the quality of life was better, comparatively. What mystifies me is why the need has not yet been felt in Japan to bring basic life standards up to the level of other countries?

ML: A different question: How come you never studied Zen or any of those Eastern philosophies?

BK: I was never interested in Zen, karate, flower arrangement or tea ceremony. The deepest insight I got into Japan was through learning the *kanji*. I struggled over kanji but I can still read them very easily. I'm lazy but I can read any sign and almost any newspaper headline. I can look at something and I know what it is. But I'm too lazy to read through a long article or book. The marvelous thing about being able to read kanji is that you can skim and get the main points of an article. The key kanji jump up at you off the page.

ML: Many Americans studied Zen Buddhism and it helped them adjust to living in Japan and understand the Japanese.

BK: That's nonsense. I think, though, that a journalist should of course know as much as possible. But those things are really not part of modern Japan and most Japanese know even less about it than many foreigners. Japanese culture is a very feminine culture. Those foreigners who study Zen, or who are into that, at least among men, are usually rather feminine men. As an aside, this is a society that attracts

170

many homosexuals. One, homosexuals are sensitive people and there are so many things in Japanese culture—beauty, material, flowers and things like that—that homosexuals are sensitive to and interested in. Maybe those are bad generalizations, but the other thing is that Japan is rather tolerant of sexual deviation; you can be a homosexual here and not really suffer; it's not an issue. People don't write about that; they write about people's mistresses but they don't write about a man being homosexually inclined. It's not interesting, it doesn't sell newspapers.

I've been to temples, and I often talked to Shiko Munakata—he was one of my favorite people. We talked about Zen but it didn't interest me. As a journalist I was always looking toward discovering new things and not delving too deeply into one subject. When I first came to Japan, there was so much to discover about the country, what they were doing, and also doing well, and where they were heading. The fact that the Japanese produced chocolate was news and also that they had "hidden Christians." There were wonderful little things you could write about in those days—about *ninja*. And then, suddenly, Japan became an economic power. If I had known in those days that this would happen, I might not have been drawn here so easily; it was not what attracted me to Japan. It was the Lafcadio Hearn aspect that brought me here. But, then, unbeknownst to me, suddenly they got to be a major economic power and I had to learn economics, something I had never expected to.

ML: And business reporting and all that other kind of stuff.

BK: Exactly—textile negotiations. I mean, it bored me actually.

ML: Well, don't you think in a sense that's one of the dangers of the future, that Japan is going to be left now to the business and the technical specialists, the economic writers, the technology writers?

BK: Yes. And also that it has lost its charm as a story.

ML: And feature writers will only write about plastic

sushi. Well, I guess that's also one of the signs that Japan has grown up.

BK: I remember working so hard to get a story about cars into *Newsweek*. We finally did it in 1968 or so. I got the business editors to agree reluctantly to run a two column story about the Japanese auto industry. And four or five years later we did a cover story on Toyota. The first efforts to write about Japanese cars were rejected. They didn't fit the stereotype; it wasn't the kind of story they expected from Japan.

ML: You know a lot is being written about Japan in the year 2000. Where do you think are the pitfalls for Japan on the way? For instance, do you see them heading down any wrong roads or right roads, are mis-steps possible?

BK: The Japanese usually pursue a goal and follow a set direction without much deviation. They set a goal and then pursue it with blinders. They did that before the war, when they set themselves on a military path. They did nothing except push to conquer neighboring countries, colonialize their neighbors, and try to beat the United States in war. And, when they failed, they totally gave up, until somebody provided another goal, economic prosperity; they've been pursuing that one pretty well ever since.

I believe whatever goal the Japanese choose to pursue will be pursued blindly until it proves to be a failure and so I believe this goal will just continue to be pursued until some threat— hopefully not—moves them in another direction. Thus, Japan basically will continue to be an economic power as long as they continue to be allowed to live in a sort of greenhouse or hot-house of US protection. That is, so long as they are closely allied to the United States, under a US nuclear umbrella, and enjoying free trade where markets will remain open for their products. Then I don't see why Japan cannot continue on this path forever. However, if things change, if the United States weakens its support of Japan, if protectionism slams the gates shut, other countries gang up on Japan, if there is too much psychological

Bernard Krisher

pressure, then there could be a drastic change. If you push the Japanese into a corner, they could react neurotically, they might be capable of a sharp ninety degree turn, and this could be anything. That's why I am always afraid of what could happen if the world situation vis-a-vis Japan changed abruptly and unexpectedly.

ML: What kind of threat?

BK: Well, in '73, there was such a threat in the possibility of a cut in their oil supply. And if that had happened, if the oil supply had stopped, if Japan had been down to one week of oil—you know, they only have reserves for up to about sixty or ninety days—if those ships ever stopped coming, if the Malacca Straits ever got bottled up, then the Japanese could move very drastically.

I understand that Nakasone, who was MITI Minister in 1973, had proposed that Japan cut relations with Israel as a means of placating the Arabs to assure their oil supply but he was vetoed or persuaded by some wiser fellows, including his career vice-minister, Eme Yamashita, to abandon that idea.

Japan has rarely moved internally; the major changes in the society have always come through external pressure—the black ships of Admiral Perry brought about the end of seclusion and ushered in the Meiji era; the defeat in 1945 took them off a military course and set them onto an economic one, and another external threat could move Japan again in still another direction. Japan is indeed a fragile place.

Biographical Notes

JAMES C. ABEGGLEN

James C. Abegglen, the author and co-author of ten books on Japan, is an eminent business consultant and also professor and director of the Graduate School of Comparative Culture at Sophia University. A graduate of Harvard and the University of Chicago, Dr. Abegglen taught at the University of Chicago and MIT. During World War II he served with the Third Marines in the Pacific and first came to Japan in 1945 with the US Strategic Bombing survey. He returned to Japan in 1955 to study Japanese industrial organization and personnel practices—the first such research into modern Japanese corporations by a Western specialist. Since that pioneering work, Dr. Abegglen has spent more than half of his time in Japan as corporate executive, management consultant and professor. The best known of his books are his classic original study of Japanese corporate organization, *The Japanese Factory*, 1958; *Big Business in America*, 1955, and, most recently, *Kaisha, the Japanese Corporation*, 1985. Dr. Abegglen was vice president and director of the Boston Consulting Group from 1965 to 1984 and founded that firm's Tokyo subsidiary. He continues as consultant to the Boston Consulting Group, while operating his own company, Asia Advisory Service, Inc., with offices in Boston and Tokyo.

ARIFIN BEY

Arifin Bey was born in Sumatra (Indonesia) in 1925. He came to Japan as a scholarship student during the Pacific War, when Indonesia was under Japanse occupation, and found himself in Hiroshima in 1945 when the city was hit by an atomic bomb from which he survived. In 1961, he completed his studies at Georgetown University, earning a Ph.D in international political science. From 1961-67 he

175

was editor of the *Indonesian Herald*, an English-language daily. He was assigned as a councillor to the Indonesian Embassy in Tokyo in 1967 and subsequently moved to *RADA*, an Indonesian militarty-supported research organization, to report from Tokyo. He has also taught at Tsukuba University in Japan and is now vice-chancellor of Bun Hatta University in Indonesia. He is the author of *The Indonesian Mind*.

ROBERT CHRISTOPHER

Robert Christopher's first encounter with a Japan, then in ruins, was as a member of the occupation forces that landed in Japan in September 1945 just a few days after Douglas MacArthur accepted the surrender of the imperial Japanese government on the battleship *Missouri*. Since then he has returned frequently as a journalist and author, witnessing Japan's miraculous reconstruction and the accompanying political and social change. Christopher was a senior editor and executive editor at *Newsweek* during its golden years. He was the originator and first editor of *Newsweek International*, and, subsequently, managing editor of *GEO* magazine. Since 1981 he has been administrator of the Pulitzer Prizes and lecturer at Columbia University's Graduate School of Journalism. Christopher is a graduate of Yale University and the author of *The Japanese Mind: the Goliath Explained*, 1983.

BERNARD KRISHER

Bernard Krisher was born in Frankfurt and left Hitler-Germany in 1937 at the age of six, settling in New York with his parents before the start of World War II. Editor of his own magazine at the age of 12, Krisher edited his high school and college (Queens College) papers and subsequently worked for the *New York Herald Tribune* and the *New York World Telegram & Sun*. He spent a year doing Japanese area and language studies at Columbia University in 1961-62 as Ford Foundation Advanced International Reporting Fellow. On completion of the program Krisher joined *Newsweek's* Tokyo bureau and subsequenty became bureau chief, a post he held until 1980. In 1978, he took a year's sabbatical to be a visiting scholar and honorary research associate at Harvard University's East Asian Research Center. In 1981, Krisher moved to *Fortune* as its Tokyo correspondent and simultaneously joined *Shinchosha*, the Tokyo publishing house, as chief editorial advisor to assist in developing a new Japanese weekly magazine, *FOCUS*, which turned out to be a media phenomenon in Japan. Krisher left *Fortune* in 1983 but remains an active participant in the weekly production of *FOCUS* and other Shinchosha projects. He is a contributor to various American magazines, including *Parade*, and the author of five books, including, (with Alan Levy) *Draftee's Confidential Guide*, 1957; *Interview*, 1976; *Nihonjin ni Umarete—Toku ka? son ka?* (with Hideaki Kase), 1978; *Harvard Nikki*, 1979 and *Harvard no mita Nihon*, 1979. Krisher is a member of the Council on Foreign Relations.

MARY LORD

Mary Lord holds an honorary degree in East Asian Studies from Harvard University, where she studied Japanese language and modern history. Born in Boston, Ms. Lord spent seven years as a correspondent in *Newsweek* magazine's Washington bureau, where she covered defense and foreign affairs. She moved to Tokyo to develop a magazine about Japan, *'Zasshi'*, which, however, did not materialize.

Ms. Lord subsequently became Far East bureau chief for *U.S. News and World Report* and currently is back in Washington as the business and financial editor for *USN&WR*.

Japan as We Lived It

DONALD RICHIE

Donald Richie's romance with Japan began more than forty years ago. An ensign in the American merchant marine, he reached a Tokyo in ruins with the occupation army in 1946. Though he knew little about movies, he applied for a film critic's job on the *Pacific Stars & Stripes* and for the next two years became the GIs guide to Hollywood. At the age of twenty-four, he first met Akira Kurosawa, who was then filming *Drunken Angel*. He returned to the United States to complete university at Columbia University in New York City but moved back to Japan in 1954 to establish himself as the foremost Western expert of the Japanese film. With Joseph L. Anderson, he wrote the first and still the best introduction to the Japanese cinema, *The Japanese Film: Art and Industry*. In his own right he has published numerous books on the Japanese film and film makers as well as penetrating studies on Japan. These include, *Ozu*, 1978; *The Films of Akira Kurosawa*, 1965, 1979 and a new Japanese expanded edition in 1981; *The Japanese Movie: All Illustrated History*, 1965, 1981; *The Inland Sea*, 1971, Japanese edition, 1981; *Companions of the Holiday*, 1968, and *The Scorching Earth*, 1956, Japanese edition, 1957. From 1968 to 1973, Richie returned to New York to serve in the prestigeous post of Curator of Film at the Museum of Modern Art. He subsequently returned to Tokyo and has continued to live there since.

JOHN RODERICK

John Roderick, the dean of American correspondents in Japan, recently retired after forty-seven years with the *Associated Press*, forty of them overseas. Beginning his career as a foreign correspondent in China, he spent six months with the Chinese Communists in Yenan, where he

Biographical Notes

met and interviewed Mao Tse-tung, Liu Shao-chi, Chou En-lai and other Red leaders. After nine years in Europe he returned to Asia to cover the last stages of the French Vietminh war in Indochina. In 1956 he became *AP's* chief China Watcher, covering the mainland from Hong Kong and Tokyo. In 1971, he became one of the first American newsmen to return to Peking, accompanying the American table tennis team. In 1979 he reopened the *AP* Peking bureau after a thirty-year absence. The *AP* made him a Special Correspondent, one of six, in 1977. A former president of the Foreign Correspondents' Club of Japan, he now lives in a two hundred and fifty year old Japanese farmhouse in Kamakura, where he continues to write. He was editor in residence at the East West Center in Hawaii in 1985.

EZRA VOGEL

Born and educated in Ohio, Ezra Vogel's first encounter with Japan was in 1958 when he conducted research in Japan for a Harvard University sociology project. In 1967, he became a Harvard professor and has since served also as director of Harvard's East Asian Research Center, chairman of the Council on East Asian Studies, director of the US-Japan program, and is a member of the Joint Committee on US-Japan Relations and the Joint Committee on Japanese Studies. Prof. Vogel is a much-sought after lecturer as well as the author of numerous books, including *Japan's New Middle Class*, 1963; *Canton Under Communism*, 1969; *Japan As Number One*, 1979, and *Comeback* , 1985. He is the editor of *A Modern Introduction to the Family* (with Norman W. Bell), 1960, *and Modern Japanese Organization and Decision-Making*, 1975.

Japan as We Lived It

AMAE dependence

BONSAI a potted dwarf tree

BUNRAKU traditional Japanese puppet theater

DANCHI a public housing development

GAIJIN a foreigner; lit. outside person

GAIMUSHO Foreign Ministry

GEIHINKAN the official government guest house for visiting heads of state

GEISHA a professional beauty and entertainer at Japanese tea houses

GIRI NINJO an act performed out of a sense of duty or obligation

HAIKU a 17-syllabled poem

HANAMACHI an elevated passage way running from the stage to the rear of the theater through the audience; lit. a flower way; frequently used to describe a grand exit from a long but lately tainted career.

HANKO a seal (used in lieu of a signature on checks, documents)

HONNE one's real intentions

KABUKI the Japanese all-male classical theater

KANJI (of the Prime Minister's press club); the reporter chosen to head the group of journalists covering the Prime Minister's beat. This posts usually rotates monthly.

KAKEJIKU a hanging scroll

KIMOCHI a good feeling

KISENG (houses) a Korean-style restaurant where kiseng girls entertain. Kiseng are Korean geisha (where the tradition reportedly began). See geisha.

MATSURI a festival

MEIJI the era named after Emperor Meiji

MITSUKOSHI a leading Tokyo department store

MIZU SHOBAI geisha, cabaret hostess, people engaged in the 'floating world' of entertainment.

MOMBUSHO the Ministry of Education

MURA HACHIBU to be ostracized from the village

MUTSU Japan's first nuclear-powered merchant ship, immobilized in Mutsu Bay as it experienced difficulty finding a regular port due to the fear of fishermen that radioactivity would destroy their catch.

NAKAMA among comrades, the inner circle

NINJA a samurai who mastered the art of making himself invisible through some artifice and engaged in spying.

NOZOKI BEJA literally a 'peeping' room

OCHAZUKE boiled rice with tea poured on it

RONRI logic

RONRITEKI logical

SASHIMI sliced raw fish

SATORI spiritual awakening

SAYONARA goodbye, farewell

SENSEI teacher

SHICHIRIN a portable clay cooking stove; a clay charcoal stove

SJOJI a paper screen for sliding door

SUKIYAKI a beef dish

SUMO Japanese style wrestling

SUSHI vinegared raw fish and rice

TATAMI straw mat

TATAMAE one's official position on an issue, but not necessarily one's true inner feelings

WA harmony

YOROSHIKU ONEGAI SHIMASU expression upon leaving, lit. I leave it to your best judgement